Decisions for Health
LEVEL RED

Study Guide

HOLT, RINEHART AND WINSTON
A Harcourt Education Company
Orlando • Austin • New York • San Diego • Toronto • London

TO THE STUDENT

This Study Guide contains Concept Review worksheets, Health Inventories, Health Behavior Contracts, and Life Skills Activities. The Concept Review worksheets can be used as a pre-reading guide to help you identify the main concepts of each chapter before your initial reading. You can also use the worksheets after reading each chapter to test your understanding of the chapter's main concepts and terminology and to prepare for exams. Health Inventories can help you assess your own health and your knowledge of health topics. Life Skills Activities will allow you to practice the Life Skills. Regardless of how you and your teacher use *Decisions for Health Study Guide*, it will help you determine which topics you have learned well and which topics you need to study further.

ISBN-13: 978-0-03-099994-9
ISBN-10: 0-03-099994-4
01 02 03 04 05 170 11 10 09 08 07

Contents

Nutrition and Your Health

A Healthy Body, a Healthy Weight

Mental and Emotional Health

Managing Stress

Teens and Drugs

Infectious Diseases

Noninfectious Diseases and Disorders

Your Changing Body

Your Personal Safety

Skills Worksheet

Concept Review

Lesson: Being Healthy and Well

1. List the four parts of health.

_____

_____

_____

_____

2. Explain the difference between health and wellness.

_____

_____

_____

3. The term _____ refers to the practice of keeping clean to prevent the spread of disease.

4. A(n) _____ is a set of questions that rates your overall health.

Read each phrase. Write P for physical health, E for emotional health, M for mental health, or S for social health in the space provided.

_____ **5.** solving problems with little trouble

_____ **6.** showing respect for other people

_____ **7.** expressing emotions in healthy ways

_____ **8.** accepting your strengths and weaknesses

_____ **9.** dealing with stress effectively

_____ **10.** visiting your doctor and dentist regularly

_____ **11.** volunteering to do things for your community

_____ **12.** getting plenty of exercise

| Concept Review *continued*

Lesson: Influences on Your Health

Write the letter of the correct answer in the space provided.

_____13. Muscular dystrophy is
   a. caused by the environment.
   b. caused by an unhealthy diet.
   c. an inherited disease of the muscles.
   d. an inherited disease of the heart.

_____14. Heart disease is affected by
   a. a person's heredity.
   b. an unhealthy diet.
   c. lack of exercise.
   d. All of the above

_____15. Seasonal affective disorder is caused by
   a. tobacco smoke.
   b. not getting enough sunlight.
   c. air pollution.
   d. not getting enough exercise.

_____16. Asbestos is an environmental hazard because
   a. it damages your lungs.
   b. it causes depression.
   c. it disturbs your ability to concentrate.
   d. All of the above

17. The term _____ refers to the passing down of traits from parents to their biological child.

18. Physical traits that can be _____, or passed down, include hair, eye, and skin color.

19. The term _____ refers to all of the living and nonliving things around you.

20. Name four things that can cause an asthma attack.

_____

_____

_____

_____

Lesson: Making Good Health Choices

21. Describe the relationship between your lifestyle and your health.

_____

_____

_____

22. List four health choices that you make every day.

_____

_____

_____

_____

23. Explain how your attitude affects your health.

_____

_____

_____

24. List four ways to practice preventive healthcare.

_____

_____

_____

_____

Match the definitions with the correct term. Write the letter in the space provided. Some terms will not be used.

_____ **25.** a set of behaviors that you live by

_____ **26.** a way of acting, thinking, or feeling that causes you to make one choice over another

_____ **27.** taking steps to help prevent illness and accidents

a. preventive healthcare

b. wellness

c. attitude

d. mental health

e. lifestyle

| Concept Review *continued*

Lesson: Nine Life Skills for Better Health

Write the letter of the correct answer in the space provided.

_____**28.** Which of the following statements is NOT true?
    a. Life skills can help you deal with many kinds of situations throughout your life.
    b. By practicing life skills, you will soon find them harder to use.
    c. By practicing life skills, you can make them part of your daily life.
    d. Keeping a record of daily events can show you how well you are using the life skills.

_____**29.** To improve your social health, you should
    a. open your mind to new ideas.
    b. exercise regularly.
    c. spend quality time with others.
    d. eat properly.

Match the descriptions with the life skill. Write the letter in the space provided.

_____**30.** evaluating each of the four parts of your health

_____**31.** judging the accuracy of advertising and other media messages

_____**32.** dealing with problems and emotions in an effective way

_____**33.** deciding to do things that will give you a sense of accomplishment

_____**34.** comparing products and services based on value and quality

_____**35.** avoiding misunderstandings by expressing your feelings in a healthy way

_____**36.** making choices that are healthy and responsible

_____**37.** saying no to things that you don't want to do

_____**38.** practicing good habits, such as getting plenty of sleep

a. setting goals
b. communicating effectively
c. making good decisions
d. assessing your health
e. practicing wellness
f. coping
g. evaluating media messages
h. being a wise consumer
i. using refusal skills

Activity

Health Inventory

Health and Wellness

This checklist can help you assess how well you take responsibility for your own healthcare. Read the following statements. Then, check the appropriate box next to each statement.

always	some-times	never	
❑	❑	❑	**1.** Do you eat a balanced diet?
❑	❑	❑	**2.** Do you get regular exercise?
❑	❑	❑	**3.** Do you sleep at least 8 hours every night?
❑	❑	❑	**4.** Do you wear your seat belt when riding in a vehicle?
❑	❑	❑	**5.** Do you wear safety equipment when playing a sport?
❑	❑	❑	**6.** Do you avoid behavior that will get you into trouble?
❑	❑	❑	**7.** Do you get regular medical checkups?
❑	❑	❑	**8.** Do you get regular dental checkups?
❑	❑	❑	**9.** Do you brush and floss your teeth every day?
❑	❑	❑	**10.** Do you avoid using tobacco, alcohol, and illegal drugs?

SCORE YOURSELF

Give yourself 4 points for each *always* answer, 2 points for each *sometimes* answer, and 0 points for each *never* answer. Write your score here: _____.

40 points: Excellent—You're already doing a great job of practicing preventive healthcare.

30 to 39 points: Very good—You need to make just a few changes to take better care of your health.

20 to 29 points: Good—You're on the right track, but you need to make several lifestyle changes.

10 to 19 points: Fair—You need to take steps now to help prevent unnecessary illness and accidents.

0 to 9 points: Yikes!—Luckily, it's not too late to make the changes you need to enjoy better health.

Name _____ Class _____ Date _____

Health Behavior Contract

Health and Wellness

My Goals: I, _____, will accomplish one or more of the following goals:

I will choose one part of my health that needs improvement and make a plan to improve.

I will practice preventive healthcare.

I will master the life skill, "Practicing Wellness."

Other: _____

_____

My Reasons: By improving one part of my health, my overall wellness will be more balanced. I will prevent injury and illness to myself by practicing preventive healthcare. By mastering the life skill, "Practicing Wellness," I will improve my overall health and fitness.

Other: _____

_____

My Values: Personal values that will help me meet my goals are

_____

_____

My Plan: The actions I will take to meet my goals are

_____

_____

Evaluation: I will use my Health Journal to keep a log of actions I took to fulfill this contract. After 1 month, I will evaluate my goals. I will adjust my plan if my goals are not being met. If my goals are being met, I will consider setting additional goals.

Signed _____

Date _____

Name _____ Class _____ Date _____

Life Skills: Assessing Your Health

Lesson: Being Healthy and Well
DEVELOPING A HEALTH ASSESSMENT

A health assessment is a set of questions that rates your overall health. For this activity, pretend that you are a school nurse. Your job is to develop a health assessment for the students at your school.

Think of two yes-or-no questions that ask about each of the four parts of health. Write your questions below.

PHYSICAL HEALTH

yes   no

❑   ❑   1. _____

❑   ❑   2. _____

EMOTIONAL HEALTH

yes   no

❑   ❑   3. _____

❑   ❑   4. _____

MENTAL HEALTH

yes   no

❑   ❑   5. _____

❑   ❑   6. _____

SOCIAL HEALTH

yes   no

❑   ❑   7. _____

❑   ❑   8. _____

Now, complete the health assessment you developed. Answer each question by checking the appropriate box.

Life Skills *continued*

ANALYSIS

1. Why was it important to include questions about all four parts of health in your assessment?

   _____

   _____

   _____

2. Which parts of health are your strong points? Explain your answer.

   _____

   _____

   _____

3. In which parts of health do you have weak points? Explain your answer.

   _____

   _____

   _____

4. Do you plan to change your behavior in any way based on your health assessment? If so, what will you change?

   _____

   _____

   _____

Activity

Life Skills: Communicating Effectively

Lesson: Nine Life Skills for Better Health
AVOIDING MISUNDERSTANDINGS

It was Kim's first day at a new school. At lunch, three girls from her health class introduced themselves and asked if they could sit with her. Kim gladly said yes. She really wanted to make friends. However, as the girls began talking about the soccer team they played on and the youth group they belonged to, Kim felt left out, so she grew quiet. The next day, the girls didn't sit with her again. Later, Kim heard that they had thought she was unfriendly.

1. What did Kim want to communicate to the girls?

_____

_____

2. What did Kim actually communicate to the girls?

_____

_____

3. What could Kim have done differently to avoid this misunderstanding?

_____

_____

_____

4. Kim needs to practice her communication skills. How can she do this?

_____

_____

_____

5. How can Kim tell if she is making progress with her communication?

_____

_____

_____

Skills Worksheet

Concept Review

Lesson: Decisions and Consequences

Match the definitions with the correct term. Write the letter in the space provided.

_____ **1.** the result of a decision

_____ **2.** a consequence that harms you or others

_____ **3.** a choice you make and act upon

_____ **4.** a consequence that is neither helpful nor harmful

_____ **5.** a consequence that helps you or others

_____ **6.** a decision in which you have carefully considered the outcome of each choice

a. positive consequence

b. neutral consequence

c. negative consequence

d. consequence

e. decision

f. goal

g. good decision

7. Explain why a good decision is a responsible decision.

_____

_____

8. Explain the difference between a positive consequence and a negative consequence.

_____

_____

_____

Lesson: Six Steps to Making Good Decisions

9. Your _____ are the beliefs that you consider to be of great importance.

10. Your _____ is the way that you think, feel, and act.

11. Your _____ are the different choices that you can make.

12. A process called _____ involves thinking of all the possible ways to carry out your decision.

| Concept Review *continued*

Number these decision-making steps in the correct order.

_____ **13.** Consider your values.

_____ **14.** Decide, and act.

_____ **15.** Evaluate your choice.

_____ **16.** Identify the problem.

_____ **17.** List the options.

_____ **18.** Weigh the consequences.

19. Explain how your values influence your decisions.

_____

_____

_____

20. Explain why you should look at the benefits and risks of your options.

_____

_____

_____

21. Explain why you should evaluate your decisions.

_____

_____

_____

Lesson: Influences on Your Decisions

Write the letter of the correct answer in the space provided.

_____ **22.** Which of the following influences your life?
   a. family values
   b. cultural beliefs
   c. family traditions
   d. All of the above

_____ **23.** Which of the following is NOT an example of peer pressure?
   a. doing something because another student talks you into it
   b. doing something because you think everyone else is doing it
   c. doing something because it is what you really want to do
   d. doing something because it is what your friends want you to do

| Concept Review *continued*

_____**24.** Which of the following statements is NOT true?
    a. All of the information you get from the media is correct.
    b. The media gives you messages about what is good and bad.
    c. Advertisers want you to identify with their products.
    d. Commercials sometimes provide misinformation.

Match the definitions with the correct term. Write the letter in the space provided.

_____**25.** pressure to do something that will
benefit you or someone else

_____**26.** TV, radio, the Internet, movies,
magazines, music, and news reports

_____**27.** someone about the same age as you are
with whom you interact

_____**28.** a feeling that you should do something
that your friends want you to do

_____**29.** pressure to do something that could
harm you or others

a. positive peer pressure

b. negative peer pressure

c. peer pressure

d. peer

e. media

30. Explain how your decisions may change based on new information.

_____

_____

_____

Lesson: Setting Healthy Goals

31. Explain why goals are important.

_____

_____

32. Explain the difference between long-term goals and short-term goals.

_____

_____

_____

33. Explain how goals help build healthy relationships.

_____

_____

Match the definitions with the correct term. Write the letter in the space provided.

_____**34.** the way you value, respect, and feel confident about yourself

_____**35.** a task that may take months or even years to accomplish

_____**36.** something that you enjoy and want to learn more about

_____**37.** a task that you can accomplish in hours, days, or weeks

_____**38.** an important belief that develops over time

_____**39.** something you work toward and hope to achieve

a. short-term goal
b. long-term goal
c. goal
d. self-esteem
e. value
f. interest

In the blanks provided, write *V* beside the phrases that describe values. Write *I* beside the phrases that describe interests.

_____**40.** usually develop over a long time

_____**41.** can start quickly and end just as fast

_____**42.** reflect your personality and tastes

_____**43.** reflect the kind of person you want to be

_____**44.** reflect your character

Lesson: How to Reach Your Goals

45. The term _____ means the achievement of your goal.

46. The term _____ means the commitment to keep working toward your goal even when you want to quit.

47. Explain how goals and success are related.

_____

_____

_____

48. Explain how mistakes can be valuable.

_____

_____

_____

Lesson: Changing Your Goals

49. Explain why it is important to measure your progress toward a goal.

_____

_____

_____

_____

50. Explain why changing your plan is sometimes part of reaching your goal.

_____

_____

_____

_____

51. Explain what *coping* means.

_____

_____

_____

_____

| Concept Review *continued*

Lesson: Skills for Success

In the blanks provided, write *L* beside the phrases that describe listening skills. Write *R* beside the phrases that describe refusal skills.

_____**52.** making eye contact

_____**53.** paying attention to the person who is speaking

_____**54.** avoiding dangerous situations

_____**55.** walking away

_____**56.** nodding when you understand

_____**57.** standing your ground

_____**58.** asking questions when you don't understand

_____**59.** saying no

_____**60.** staying focused on the problem

61. A skill called _____ is the ability to exchange information and express thoughts and feelings clearly.

62. Strategies called _____ are ways to avoid doing something you don't want to do.

63. A(n) _____ question calls for an answer other than yes or no.

64. Explain why communication is important.

_____

_____

_____

_____

Name _____ Class _____ Date _____

Successful Decisions and Goals

Read the following statements. Think about how well each one describes your behavior. Then, check the appropriate box.

often | some-times | rarely

☐ ☐ ☐   **1.** How often do you make a choice without thinking it through?

☐ ☐ ☐   **2.** How often do you later regret a decision that you have made?

☐ ☐ ☐   **3.** How often do your decisions lead to negative consequences for yourself or others?

☐ ☐ ☐   **4.** How often have you done something because a friend did it first, and then only later regretted doing that action ?

☐ ☐ ☐   **5.** How often have you done something you didn't want to do because a friend talked you into it?

☐ ☐ ☐   **6.** How often have you bought something you didn't need because of an advertisement?

☐ ☐ ☐   **7.** How often do feel as if you don't know what your goals are?

☐ ☐ ☐   **8.** How often do you feel as if you aren't making enough progress toward your goals?

☐ ☐ ☐   **9.** How often do you feel as if you have trouble making decisions?

SCORE YOURSELF

Give yourself 0 points for each *often* answer, 2 points for each *sometimes* answer, and 4 points for each *rarely* answer.

Write your score here: _____.

30–36: Excellent—You do a great job of making wise decisions and setting good goals.

20–29: Good—You often do a good job when it comes to your decisions and goals.

10–19: Fair—You could stand to improve your decision-making and goal-setting skills.

0–9: You need to work on learning to make successful decisions and set effective goals.

Activity

Health Behavior Contract

Successful Decisions and Goals

My Goals: I, _____, will accomplish one or more of the following goals:

I will set a long-term goal and will list the steps I will take to reach that goal.

I will practice making decisions by using the six steps to making good decisions.

I will practice using the five refusal skills.

Other: _____

_____

My Reasons: By knowing the steps that I need to take, I will be able to reach a goal that I set. By using the six steps to making good decisions, I will be able to make responsible decisions. By practicing refusal skills, I will be prepared to say no to something that I do not want to do.

Other: _____

_____

My Values: Personal values that will help me meet my goals are

_____

_____

_____

My Plan: The actions I will take to meet my goals are

_____

_____

_____

Evaluation: I will use my Health Journal to keep a log of actions I took to fulfill this contract. After 1 month, I will evaluate my goals. I will adjust my plan if my goals are not being met. If my goals are being met, I will consider setting additional goals.

Signed _____

Date _____

Activity

Life Skills: Setting Goals

Lesson: Setting Healthy Goals
ACHIEVING LONG-TERM GOALS

Long-term goals may take months or even years to achieve. Usually, they are made up of several short-term goals and even other long-term goals. For example, suppose that your long-term goal is to become a doctor. In this activity, you'll look at some of the steps you would need to take to make this goal a reality.

1. To be a doctor, you have to go to college. What is one goal you might set for yourself five years from now?

_____

_____

_____

2. To get into college, you need to make good grades in high school. What is one goal you might set for yourself three years from now?

_____

_____

_____

3. To succeed in high school, you need to be well prepared in middle school. What is one goal you might set for yourself next year?

_____

_____

4. To succeed in middle school, you need to have good study skills. What is one goal you might set for yourself this year?

_____

_____

_____

5. To develop good study skills, you need to do your homework. What is one goal you might set for yourself tonight?

_____

_____

_____

Activity

Life Skills: Communicating Effectively

Lesson: Skills for Success
GOOD LISTENING SKILLS

Courtney has agreed to take care of her friend Bill's hamster while he and his family go on vacation. The day before he leaves, Bill brings the hamster over to Courtney's house. He explains about feeding it, giving it water, and cleaning its cage. Courtney is staring out the window, but she's listening. So she is surprised when Bill suddenly seems annoyed. "If you don't care enough to pay attention," he says, "I'll find somebody else to take care of my hamster."

1. What could Courtney have done differently to show that she was interested in what Bill was saying?

_____

_____

2. Courtney understood Bill's instructions for cleaning the hamster cage. How could she have shown this?

_____

_____

3. Courtney wasn't quite sure how often she was supposed to feed the hamster. What should she have done?

_____

_____

_____

4. Why is it important to develop good listening skills?

_____

_____

_____

Skills Worksheet

Concept Review

Lesson: Self-Esteem and Your Life

In the blanks provided, write *H* beside the sentences that describe someone who has high self-esteem. Write *L* beside the sentences that describe someone who has low self-esteem.

_____ 1. Carla is afraid to try anything new because she thinks people might laugh at her if she makes a mistake.

_____ 2. Dave has very little self-confidence.

_____ 3. Layla is always smiling and friendly. She's the kind of person that others want to be around.

_____ 4. All through class, Ellis stares down at his notebook. When the teacher calls on him, he usually shrugs his shoulders and turns red in the face.

_____ 5. The entire class laughed at Lily when she tripped on stage. Lily turned to the class, smiled, and curtsied.

_____ 6. Bianca is no math whiz. She has to work a little harder than others, but that's okay. She knows that people are smart in different ways. Her strong subjects are reading and writing.

_____ 7. Every Tuesday and Thursday, Janiqua goes to the library after lunch. She's been tutoring another student there for the past six weeks.

_____ 8. Joseph is depressed. As a matter of fact, it seems that he is nearly always depressed. He rarely can find the positive in a situation.

_____ 9. Logan's friend dares him to shoplift something to prove he has "guts." Logan refuses, saying that he doesn't need to prove anything to anyone who would ask him to do something he knows is wrong.

10. How might negative comments affect someone with low self-esteem?

_____

_____

11. How might negative comments affect someone with high self-esteem?

_____

_____

12. How might positive comments affect someone with low self-esteem?

_____

_____

Lesson: Your Self-Concept

In the blanks provided, write *A* beside the sentences that relate to academic self-concept. Write *S* beside the sentences that relate to social self-concept. Write *P* beside the sentences that relate to physical self-concept.

_____**13.** Sara wishes she had long, straight hair instead of her curly hair.

_____**14.** Malik is outgoing and friendly.

_____**15.** Anthony won the poetry contest last month.

_____**16.** Samarra is embarrassed by her hand-me-down, out-of-style jacket.

_____**17.** Phil did not pass his last two history tests.

_____**18.** Janika is a starter on the basketball team.

_____**19.** Laurence always sits by himself during lunch.

_____**20.** Fiona is the tallest person in her class.

_____**21.** David is on the math team.

22. What is self-esteem?

_____

_____

23. What is self-concept?

_____

_____

24. How does a positive self-concept lead to high self-esteem?

_____

_____

_____

_____

| Concept Review *continued*

Lesson: Keys to Healthy Self-Esteem

In the blanks provided, write *YES* beside the behaviors that can build healthy self-esteem. Write *NO* beside the behaviors that can lower self-esteem.

_____ **25.** lying to your parents

_____ **26.** taking responsibility for a mistake

_____ **27.** working to improve your science grade

_____ **28.** telling yourself that you can do it

_____ **29.** practicing good hygiene; making sure your appearance is neat and clean

_____ **30.** gossiping about a friend

_____ **31.** spending all your time watching TV

_____ **32.** expecting that you will fail

_____ **33.** never trying anything new

_____ **34.** making sure your chores are done

35. What does being *assertive* mean?

_____

_____

_____

36. How can self-talk affect your self-esteem?

_____

_____

_____

_____

Activity

Health Inventory

Building Self-Esteem

Read each statement below. Decide whether it describes you. Write *always*, *sometimes*, or *never* in the space to the left of each statement.

_____ **1.** I can do many different things.

_____ **2.** There are things that I really like about myself.

_____ **3.** I know the kind of person I want to be.

_____ **4.** There are people in my life whom I admire.

_____ **5.** I think about how my decisions affect my future.

_____ **6.** I have friends and family members who care about me.

_____ **7.** I like the way I look.

_____ **8.** I can control many things in my life.

_____ **9.** I can resist peer pressure when I'm faced with difficult decisions.

_____ **10.** I respect myself.

Score yourself: Give yourself 3 points for each *always* answer, 1 point for each *sometimes*, and 0 for each *never*. Write your score here _____.

21–30: You have a high level self-esteem.
12–20: You have average or moderate self-esteem.
0–11: You may have an unhealthy level of self-esteem.

Name _____ Class _____ Date _____

Activity

Health Behavior Contract

Building Self-Esteem

My Goals: I, _____, will accomplish one or more of the following goals:

I will build a higher level of self-esteem.

I will make the three keys of self-esteem part of my character.

I will concentrate on my strengths and make a plan to overcome my weaknesses.

Other: _____

_____

My Reasons: By improving my self-esteem, I will improve my overall character and attitude. I will feel good about myself as a person, and I will have more confidence.

Other: _____

_____

My Values: Personal values that will help me meet my goals are

_____

_____

_____

My Plan: The actions I will take to meet my goals are

_____

_____

_____

Evaluation: I will use my Health Journal to keep a log of actions I took to fulfill this contract. After 1 month, I will evaluate my goals. I will adjust my plan if my goals are not being met. If my goals are being met, I will consider setting additional goals.

Signed _____

Date _____

Name _____ Class _____ Date _____

Life Skills: Assessing Your Health

Lesson: Self-Esteem and Your Life
BEING A GOOD FRIEND

Friends can make life happier, safer, and more interesting. Friends can share ideas, give advice, teach new skills, offer compassion and acceptance, and make us laugh. Being a good friend can boost your self-esteem and the self-esteem of your friends.

Are you a good friend? Read each statement below. Decide if the statement describes you. Write *always, sometimes,* or *never* in the space to the left of each statement.

_____ **1.** I listen when my friends are talking.

_____ **2.** I encourage my friends when they are uncertain.

_____ **3.** I am honest. My friends can trust me.

_____ **4.** I respect my friends.

_____ **5.** I don't put my friends down.

_____ **6.** I can compromise with my friends.

_____ **7.** My friends can count on me.

_____ **8.** I laugh with my friends.

_____ **9.** I don't ask my friends to do anything that could harm them.

_____ **10.** I care about my friends.

Give yourself 2 points for each *always* answer, 1 point for each *sometimes* answer, and 0 points for each *never* answer. The closer you score to 20, the better friend you are. If you scored 1 or 0 points on any item, you might want to work on that area.

11. What qualities do you look for in a friend?

_____

_____

_____

Name _____ Class _____ Date _____

Life Skills: Practicing Wellness

Lesson: Keys to Healthy Self-Esteem
LEARN TO RELAX

Taking time to relax can have several benefits. It can help relieve stress. It gives you an opportunity to get in touch with yourself. It can help you tune out negative comments and situations. It gives you a space to replace these negative thoughts with positive thoughts.

Below are several techniques you can use to relax. Try each one to find which works best for you. Remember that relaxing is a skill; you will have to practice to be good at it.

Progressive Relaxation

Start with your head or your toes. Tighten that part of your body for 3-5 seconds and then slowly relax it. Repeat this, moving up or down your body. If you started with your head, move down to your neck, shoulders, and so on. If you started with your toes, move up to your feet, ankles, calves, and so on.

Another way to practice progressive relaxation is to imagine your body parts getting warm.

Meditation

Learning to meditate usually requires a quiet place where you can be alone. Once you've learned the techniques, you'll be able to meditate almost anywhere.

Close your eyes. Breathe normally. Don't try to control your breathing, but concentrate on it. Notice the rate and rhythm. Pay attention to how your breathing changes. Practice for 10–15 minutes.

Visualization

Close your eyes. Imagine a relaxing place. If you enjoy relaxing at the beach, create a beach scene. If a walk in the park is relaxing for you, create a park scene. Imagine the sights, sounds, and smells. Stay in your relaxing place for several minutes, until you feel calm and relaxed.

Skills Worksheet

Concept Review

Lesson: The Parts of Fitness

Match each definition to the correct term. Write the correct letter in the space provided.

_____ **1.** type of endurance that keeps you from becoming short of breath

_____ **2.** the amount of force that muscles apply when they are used

_____ **3.** ability to do everyday activities without becoming short of breath, sore, or tired

_____ **4.** the ability to bend and twist joints easily

_____ **5.** compares the weight of fat in the body to the weight of muscles, bones, and organs

_____ **6.** ability of muscles to keep working over time

_____ **7.** ability to do activities for more than a few minutes

a. physical fitness

b. flexibility

c. heart and lung endurance

d. muscular endurance

e. body composition

f. endurance

g. strength

8. Explain why you should exercise.

_____

_____

9. List healthy fitness zones for your age group.

_____

_____

10. Describe how to use FIT without causing injury.

_____

_____

11. How are resting heart rate and recovery time related?

_____

_____

_____

| Concept Review *continued*

Lesson: Energy for Exercise

For each activity, write *A* for aerobic and *AN* for anaerobic. Some activities may use both.

_____**12.** sprinting 100 meters

_____**13.** lifting weights

_____**14.** playing tennis

_____**15.** running a marathon

_____**16.** swimming a mile

Lesson: Sports and Competition

17. What are five characteristics of a good sport?

_____

_____

_____

_____

_____

18. What are two ways you can get involved in sports?

_____

_____

Lesson: Weight Training

19. Describe four weight-training exercises.

_____

_____

_____

_____

_____

_____

_____

_____

| Concept Review *continued*

20. List seven weight-training rules.

_____

_____

_____

_____

_____

_____

Lesson: Injury

21. List six warning signs of injury.

_____

_____

_____

_____

_____

_____

22. List five signs of overtraining.

_____

_____

_____

_____

_____

Concept Review *continued*

Lesson: Common Injuries

In the blanks provided, write *acute* if the condition is an acute injury or *chronic* if the condition is a chronic injury.

_____ **23.** fracture

_____ **24.** tendinitis

_____ **25.** sprain

_____ **26.** stress fracture

27. Describe the steps of RICE.

_____

_____

_____

_____

_____

_____

_____

Lesson: Eight Ways to Avoid Injury

28. List eight ways to avoid injury.

_____

_____

_____

_____

_____

_____

_____

_____

_____

Activity

Health Inventory

Physical Fitness

Read each statement below. Decide whether it describes how you take responsibility for your physical fitness. Write *always*, *sometimes*, or *never* in the space to the left of each statement.

_____ **1.** I am careful to use correct form when exercising.

_____ **2.** I make time to do a warm-up and cool-down when I exercise.

_____ **3.** I am aware that physical activity can improve body composition.

_____ **4.** I try to exercise longer to improve my fitness.

_____ **5.** After exercising, I check my heart rate to see if it is in my target zone.

_____ **6.** I practice good sportsmanship when participating in sports.

_____ **7.** I incorporate weight training, aerobic activity, and stretching in my exercise work-outs.

_____ **8.** I follow safety rules while weight-lifting.

_____ **9.** I pay attention to warning signs of injury and, if necessary, seek treatment.

_____ **10.** I rarely spend long periods of time watching TV, playing video games, or using a computer.

Score yourself: Give yourself 4 points for each always answer, 2 points for each sometimes answer, and 0 points for each never. Write your score here _____.

36–40: Excellent—You have a safe and effective physical program.
26–35: Good—You are developing a safe and effective physical fitness program.
20–25: Fair—You should improve your physical fitness program.
Fewer than 20: You should develop a physical fitness program right away.

Name _____ Class _____ Date _____

Health Behavior Contract

Physical Fitness

My Goals: I, _____, will accomplish one or more of the following goals:

I will improve my physical fitness.

I will exercise at least three times a week.

I will test my fitness regularly.

Other: _____

_____

My Reasons: Exercise will improve my physical fitness. It will keep me from becoming short of breath, sore, and tired easily. Improving my fitness also keeps me from getting diseases such as heart disease, diabetes, and obesity. If I exercise regularly, I may live a longer life.

Other: _____

_____

My Values: Personal values that will help me meet my goals are

_____

_____

_____

My Plan: The actions I will take to meet my goals are

_____

_____

_____

Evaluation: I will use my Health Journal to keep a log of actions I took to fulfill this contract. After 1 month, I will evaluate my goals. I will adjust my plan if my goals are not being met. If my goals are being met, I will consider setting additional goals.

Signed _____

Date _____

Activity

Life Skills: Communicating Effectively

Lesson: Your Fitness Program
FITNESS IN A BUSY FAMILY

Read the following situation and answer the questions in the space provided.

Mr. and Mrs. Spinoza have two teenage children. They want their children to be healthy and fit. The Spinozas are concerned that their busy schedules, fast food, TV, and video games may make this difficult. How can the Spinozas let their children know about their concerns?

1. How do video games, junk food, and TV make it tough for kids to be physically fit? What could the Spinozas do about this?

_____

_____

_____

_____

_____

2. How can busy schedules make it tough for kids to be physically fit? What could the Spinozas do about this?

_____

_____

_____

_____

_____

_____

3. How can the Spinozas encourage their children to be fit?

_____

_____

_____

_____

Name _____ Class _____ Date _____

Life Skills: Being a Wise Consumer

Lesson: Weight Training
EVALUATING ADVERTISING

Read the advertisement and complete the questions.

> **BODYBUILDING**
> **SUPPLEMENTS**
> **PACK ON THE MUSCLE!**
> **HUGE SELECTIONS OF**
> **BODYBUILDING SUPPLEMENTS**
> **ARE IN STOCK AND READY**
> **TO SHIP NOW!**
> **CHOOSE FROM SUPPLEMENT "X" TO LOSE WEIGHT,**
> **SUPPLEMENT "A" TO GAIN WEIGHT, OR**
> **SUPPLEMENT "C" TO GAIN SIZE AND STRENGTH**
> **WORLD'S MOST POTENT SUPPLEMENTS!**
> **100% SATISFACTION GUARANTEED!**

1. Does this ad give you enough information about these products? What information is missing?

_____

_____

_____

2. What do you know about the safety of these supplements?

_____

_____

_____

3. Should these supplements be included in your weight-training program? Why or why not?

_____

_____

Skills Worksheet

Concept Review

Lesson: Nutrition and Diet

Write the letter of the correct answer in the space provided.

_____ **1.** Nutrition is
  a. the type of foods you eat.
  b. the amount of food you eat.
  c. the study of how our body uses food.
  d. the study of your body and its functions.

2. How does nutrition affect your overall health?

_____

_____

_____

3. Name three possible consequences of eating too little food.

_____

_____

_____

In the blanks provided, fill in the letters of the terms being described.

4. process of breaking food down into usable energy: D __ __ E __ T __ __ __

5. nutrients turned into usable energy: __ E __ __ __ O __ __ S __

6. substances found in food: __ __ T __ __ E __ __ __

7. In the blanks provided, fill in numbers to put the following steps of digestion in the correct order.

_____ Nutrients are absorbed and sent to the tissues of the body.

_____ You chew your food and swallow it.

_____ Food passes into the small intestine and is broken into nutrients.

_____ Food passes into stomach and is broken down into a thick liquid.

Concept Review *continued*

8. Does every food have every nutrient? Explain your answer.

_____

_____

_____

9. A pattern of eating that includes what you eat, how much you eat, and how
often you eat is called _____.

10. List the six factors that affect your food choices.

_____

_____

_____

_____

11. How might eating because of your feelings be unhealthy?

_____

_____

_____

Lesson: The Six Classes of Essential Nutrients

12. What kind of nutrients do you get from food?

_____

_____

13. Name three classes of nutrients that are direct sources of energy.

_____

_____

14. Name two classes of nutrients that control many body functions.

_____

_____

15. Which nutrient transports the other nutrients throughout your body?

_____

| Concept Review *continued*

Match each food in the right column with the nutrient it supplies in the left column. Write the letter in the space provided.

_____ **16.** carbohydrates

_____ **17.** protein

_____ **18.** vitamins

_____ **19.** fats

a. butter
b. fish
c. pasta
d. strawberries

In the blanks provided, fill in the letters of the terms being described.

20. needed to build strong bones: C __ __ C __ __ __

21. helps regulate blood pressure: __ __ T __ __ __ I __ M

22. gum disease from a lack of vitamin: __ __ U R __ Y

23. dry out from lack of fluids: D __ __ Y __ __ __ T __

Lesson: Balancing Your Diet

24. What three tools have been developed to help you make healthy food choices?

_____

_____

25. The Dietary Guidelines for Americans recommend minimizing the intake of which food items?

_____

26. Identify the food group or type represented by each stripe in the MyPyramid symbol below.

a. _____

b. _____

c. _____

d. _____

e. _____

f. _____

a.   b.   c. d. e.   f.

Concept Review *continued*

27. What does the width of each stripe in the MyPyramid symbol represent?

_____

_____

_____

_____

28. Identify the three parts of the Nutrition Facts label shown here.

_____ **a.**

_____ **b.**   **a.** ——

_____ **c.**   **b.** ——

Nutrition Facts		
Serving Size 1 cup (252g)		
Servings per Container 2		
Amount per Serving		
Calories 180		Calories from Fat 30
		%Daily Value
Total Fat 1g		2%
Saturated Fat 0.5g		3%
Trans Fat 0g		
Cholesterol		1%
Sodium 880mg		37%
Total Carbohydrate 13g		4%
Dietary Fiber 3g		12%
Sugars 15g		
Protein 6g		
Vitamin A		15%
Vitamin C		10%
Vitamin D		10%
Calcium		15%
Iron		15%
Thiamin		10%
Riboflavin		15%
Niacin		15%
Folic Acid		25%

c.

29. A _____ is a standard amount of food that allows foods to be compared with one another.

30. Describe the difference between a portion and a serving size.

_____

_____

_____

_____

Lesson: Building Healthful Eating Habits

31 Name two effects of not eating breakfast.

_____

_____

32. List three ways of choosing good snacks.

_____

_____

_____

_____

33. Name three ways you can eat healthfully at a fast-food restaurant.

_____

_____

_____

_____

34. Healthy meals can be made at home following suggestions from the

_____ and the MyPyramid food guidance system.

Name _____ Class _____ Date _____

Health Inventory

Nutrition and Your Health

Read each statement below. Decide whether it describes how often you practice healthy eating habits. Write *always*, *sometimes,* or *never* on the line provided.

_____ **1.** I drink 8 to 10 glasses of water every day.

_____ **2.** I eat a healthy breakfast every morning.

_____ **3.** I choose healthy snacks.

_____ **4.** I eat regular size fast-food meals.

_____ **5.** I eat the recommended amounts of fruits and vegetables.

_____ **6.** I look for healthy snack foods that taste good.

_____ **7.** I eat only when I'm hungry.

_____ **8.** I eat small portions of high-fat foods.

_____ **9.** I try to eat healthy foods when I'm sad.

_____ **10.** I eat the recommended amounts of foods from the grains group and the meat and beans group.

Score Yourself: Give yourself 3 points for each *always* answer, 1 point for each sometimes, and 0 for each never. Write your score here:_____.

25–30 Excellent—You're in the habit of eating healthy! Keep up the good work.
19–24 Good—You're on your way. Stay focused.
13–18 Fair—You're starting to make some good food choices. Keep trying.
Fewer than 13—You've got to try harder!

Activity

Health Behavior Contract

Nutrition and Your Health

My Goals: I, _____, will accomplish one or more of the following goals:

I will improve my overall nutrition.

I will learn to prepare healthful meals for myself at home.

I will make healthy food choices when I eat out.

Other: _____

_____

My Reasons: By improving my nutrition I will improve my overall health and feel confident that I am doing something good for my body. I will learn what foods are good for me and I will be able to make healthy food choices.

Other: _____

_____

My Values: Personal values that will help me meet my goals are

_____

_____

_____

My Plan: The actions I will take to meet my goals are

_____

_____

_____

Evaluation: I will use my Health Journal to keep a log of actions I took to fulfill this contract. After 1 month, I will evaluate my goals. I will adjust my plan if my goals are not being met. If my goals are being met, I will consider setting additional goals.

Signed _____

Date _____

Activity

Life Skills: Setting Goals

Lesson: The Six Classes of Essential Nutrients
CREATING A HEALTHY LIVING PLAN

Create a healthy living plan based on the Dietary Guidelines for Americans. Set a goal for following the plan, and describe the experience.

CHOOSE HEALTHY, NUTRITIOUS FOOD

Create a personalized meal plan for one week. Use the MyPyramid food guidance system when planning.

STAY FIT

Choose a physical activity that interests you, and develop a schedule for doing it.

LIMIT ITEMS THAT INCREASE DISEASE RISK

Plan to eat at least one sensible low-fat, low-sugar, or low-sodium snack per day.

Attach a copy of your personalized meal plan, your fitness plan, and your list of sensible snacks.

(Activity)

Life Skills: Being a Wise Consumer

Lesson: Balancing Your Diet
MAKING A FOOD BUDGET

Living on a budget is a way of life. Budgets include housing, utilities, and living expenses. Food expenses are included in living expenses. Pretend you have $60 budgeted for food expenses to feed two people for one week. How will you spend your money?

Budget-conscious shoppers look at sales papers and clip coupons. Look at the newspaper in your area for grocery sales ads. Consider that you must feed two people three well-balanced meals for one week. Fast-food meals must also be included in this budget. Remember to consider the MyPyramid food guidance system and the Dietary Guidelines for Americans as you select your foods. Clip the ads you use and attach them to this paper. Write down the costs of food, any coupons you could use, and your total expenses.

1. Is it cheaper to eat foods prepared at home or to buy fast-food meals?

_____

_____

_____

2. Can you afford a meal at a restaurant after buying your groceries?

_____

_____

_____

3. What could you do to stretch your money further?

_____

_____

_____

_____

4. Did you consider quantity versus cost?

_____

_____

_____

Skills Worksheet

Concept Review

Lesson: What Is Body Image?

1. Your body image is the way you _____ and

_____ your body.

2. Most teens _____ as they grow and as their bodies change.

3. How does your body image affect your life?

_____

_____

_____

4. Describe someone who has an unhealthy body image.

_____

_____

_____

Lesson: Building a Healthy Body Image

Use the terms from the following list to complete the paragraph below. A term may be used only once.

music videos	thin	movies	typical
unhealthy body image	unrealistic	TV	muscular
magazines	unattractive		

The media, which include 5. _____,

6. _____, 7. _____ and

8. _____, can influence your body image. The media often

show women and girls who are unusually 9. _____ and men

and boys who are unusually 10. _____. Some people may feel

11. _____ compared to the models and actors in the media,

but these people are not 12. _____. These

13. _____ representations of people can lead teens to

develop a(n) 14. _____.

Concept Review *continued*

15. Describe the ways other people can affect your body image.

_____

_____

_____

_____

16. Describe how using "I" statements can help you build a healthy body image.

_____

_____

_____

_____

Lesson: Eating Disorders

In the blanks provided, write *U* beside the items that describe an unhealthy eating behavior. Write *H* beside the items that describe healthy eating behaviors.

_____ **17.** fad diets

_____ **18.** eating a variety of foods

_____ **19.** skipping meals

_____ **20.** bingeing

_____ **21.** following a healthy diet

_____ **22.** fasting

_____ **23.** eating well-balanced meals

_____ **24.** using diet pills

_____ **25.** eating only certain foods

_____ **26.** purging

Concept Review *continued*

Complete the chart by identifying symptoms and consequences of each eating disorder.

EATING DISORDER	SYMPTOMS (give at least 3 for each)	CONSEQUENCES (give at least 3 for each)
Anorexia Nervosa	27.	28.
Bulimia Nervosa	29.	30.
Binge Eating Disorder	31.	32.

33. Describe five possible causes of eating disorders.

_____

_____

_____

_____

_____

Lesson: Managing Your Weight

34. How can you determine your healthy weight range?

_____

_____

35. Explain why there is no ideal weight for a person.

_____

_____

_____

_____

36. Besides inherited traits, what are four factors that can affect your weight as you become an adult?

_____

_____

_____

_____

Concept Review *continued*

37. Describe the relationship between physical activity and gaining weight.

_____

_____

_____

38. Describe the relationship between physical activity and losing weight.

_____

_____

_____

39. Describe the relationship between physical activity and maintaining weight.

_____

_____

_____

_____

40. Explain how emotions can affect your eating behaviors.

_____

_____

_____

41. List six situations that might affect what and how you eat.

_____

_____

_____

_____

_____

_____

Concept Review *continued*

In the blanks provided, write _G_ beside the items that are good nutritional choices. Write _N_ beside the items that are not good nutritional choices.

_____ **42.** fresh fruits

_____ **43.** cake

_____ **44.** water

_____ **45.** lean meat

_____ **46.** juice

_____ **47.** french fries

_____ **48.** fresh vegetables

_____ **49.** potato chips

_____ **50.** soda

_____ **51.** candies

_____ **52.** chicken

53. List six things you can do to stay physically active.

_____

_____

_____

_____

_____

_____

54. What are three benefits of staying physically active?

_____

_____

_____

Name _____ Class _____ Date _____

A Healthy Body, a Healthy Weight

Decide how well each of the following statements applies to you. Read each statement and check the appropriate box.

strongly applies	applies somewhat	does not apply at all	
❑	❑	❑	**1.** I know that having a good body image will help me to have more confidence.
❑	❑	❑	**2.** I am comfortable with my body.
❑	❑	❑	**3.** I know that balancing good eating habits with physical activity can help me to manage my weight.
❑	❑	❑	**4.** I do not constantly compare myself other people.
❑	❑	❑	**5.** I understand that my body is growing and changing.
❑	❑	❑	**6.** I do not want to alter my body in any drastic ways.
❑	❑	❑	**7.** I do not pretend to eat my food.
❑	❑	❑	**8.** I do not have a great fear of gaining weight.
❑	❑	❑	**9.** I know that media images are often unrealistic.
❑	❑	❑	**10.** When people make comments that hurt my feelings, I respond with "I" statements.
❑	❑	❑	**11.** I eat a healthy, well-balanced diet.
❑	❑	❑	**12.** I understand that certain factors which I cannot control can affect my weight.
❑	❑	❑	**13.** I do not try fad diets.
❑	❑	❑	**14.** I know and understand my healthy weight range.
❑	❑	❑	**15.** I do not let my emotions control my eating behaviors.

Score yourself: Give yourself 3 points for each *strongly applies* answer, 1 point for each *applies somewhat,* and 0 for each *does not apply at all.* Write your score here _____.

34–45: Excellent—You definitely have a good body image and understand why that's important.

21–33: Good—You have a pretty good body image and understand fairly well why it's important.

10–20: Fair—You may need to work on having a better body image.

Less than 10: Learning more about body image will help you to maintain your physical and emotional health.

Name _____ Class _____ Date _____

Health Behavior Contract

A Healthy Body, a Healthy Weight

My Goals: I, _____, will accomplish one or more of the following goals:

I will improve my body image.

I will determine my healthy weight range, and with the help of my family doctor, I will devise a plan to keep my weight within that range.

I will make healthier food choices and do something active every day.

Other: _____

_____

My Reasons: By building a healthy body image, I will be able to face new challenges with confidence and feel comfortable around my friends and peers. By determining a healthy weight range and taking steps to keep my weight within that range, I will protect my overall health.

Other: _____

_____

My Values: Personal values that will help me meet my goals are

_____

_____

_____

My Plan: The actions I will take to meet my goals are

_____

_____

_____

Evaluation: I will use my Health Journal to keep a log of actions I took to fulfill this contract. After 1 month, I will evaluate my goals. I will adjust my plan if my goals are not being met. If my goals are being met, I will consider setting additional goals.

Signed _____

Date _____

Activity

Life Skills: Coping

Lesson: What Is Body Image?
LIKING YOUR BODY

As you know from reading this lesson, having a good body image is important—but can be difficult. Everywhere you look, the media bombards you with images of "perfect" bodies. It is hard to not compare yourself to actors and models you see everyday on TV and in magazines, movies, and music videos. In fact, you shouldn't compare yourself to anyone else. Remember, everyone has a different body.

Create quick reference cards to help cope with those moments.

Follow the directions below to complete the reference cards.

1. **For each scenario, think of something you could say to yourself.** This should be something that reminds you that the image you've seen is unrealistic. It should also remind you that it is important to be comfortable with the body you do have. Finally, it should remind you why a healthy body image is important. Use the example as a guide, but make your responses personal for your own use.

2. **Cut out the cards and keep them in a handy place, like your locker, schoolbag, or wallet.**

3. **Refer to the cards whenever you start to feel "down" about your body.**

EXAMPLE

> **When I start to compare myself to a magazine model with a perfect body, I can STOP and say to myself:**
>
> That is an unrealistic body image. I do not have the same body, but that's OK. I
>
> like my body the way it is. My body is changing and growing every day, and I
>
> don't mind. Liking my body the way it is will help me have more confidence.

CARD A

> **When I start to compare myself to a classmate who is thinner than I am, I can STOP and say to myself:**
>
> _____
>
> _____
>
> _____

Life Skills *continued*

CARD B

When I start to compare myself to a classmate who has bigger muscles than I do, I can STOP and say to myself:

_____

_____

_____

CARD C

When I start to compare myself to a television actor who is taller than I am, I can STOP and say to myself:

_____

_____

_____

CARD D

When I start to compare myself to a celebrity who has perfect hair and flawless skin, I can STOP and say to myself:

_____

_____

_____

Name _____ Class _____ Date _____

Life Skills: Practicing Wellness

Lesson: Managing Your Weight
PLAN A DIET

Managing your weight depends on what you eat and how much physical activity you get. The most important thing you can do to manage your weight and maintain your health is to eat balanced, nutritional meals. A diet that includes plenty of fruits and vegetables and is low in fat, salt, and sugar will help you to stay healthy and manage your weight.

Using the nutritional information on packages, and what you know about good foods—fruits, vegetables, lean meats, whole grain products, and low-fat dairy options—plan balanced, nutritional meals for five days. It may help to use the Food Guide Pyramid.

MONDAY

Breakfast: _____

_____

Lunch: _____

_____

Dinner: _____

_____

TUESDAY

Breakfast: _____

_____

Lunch: _____

_____

Dinner: _____

_____

Name _____ Class _____ Date _____

Life Skills *continued*

WEDNESDAY

Breakfast: _____

_____

Lunch: _____

_____

Dinner: _____

_____

THURSDAY

Breakfast: _____

_____

Lunch: _____

_____

Dinner: _____

_____

FRIDAY

Breakfast: _____

_____

Lunch: _____

_____

Dinner: _____

_____

Skills Worksheet

Concept Review

Lesson: Kinds of Emotions

1. Explain how teens' changing lives and bodies affect their emotions.

_____

_____

_____

2. _____ health is the way people think about and respond to events in their lives.

3. Describe how emotions can be pleasant or unpleasant.

_____

_____

4. _____ health is the way a person experiences and deals with feelings.

5. What is an *emotional spectrum?*

_____

_____

6. Define *prejudice*. _____

_____

7. Anger is an emotion of strong disappointment and _____.

8. _____ is aiming your feelings at a person who did nothing to cause those feelings.

9. List one healthy way to manage anger.

_____

_____

_____

| Concept Review *continued*

10. List five ways the body responds to fear.

_____

_____

_____

_____

_____

Lesson: Expressing Emotions

Match each item in the right column to the correct term in the left column. Write the letter of the correct answer in the space provided.

_____**11.** a way to express thoughts and emotions with the face, hands, and posture

_____**12.** expressing and understanding thoughts and emotions by talking

_____**13.** using an art to express emotion

_____**14.** not only hearing, but showing you also understand what the person is saying

a. creative expression
b. verbal communication
c. active listening
d. body language

Lesson: Managing Your Emotions

Write the letter of the correct answer in the space provided.

_____**15.** Focusing on only the bad parts of a situation is called
    a. positive self-talk.
    b. creative expression.
    c. a good way to work out your problems.
    d. negative thinking.

_____**16.** The process of thinking about the good parts of a bad situation is called
    a. positive self-talk.
    b. creative expression.
    c. a good way to work out your problems.
    d. negative thinking.

Concept Review *continued*

_____ **17.** Defense mechanisms can be healthy when
  a. they help you to avoid a stressful situation.
  b. they allow you to ignore a stressful situation.
  c. they help you deal with a stressful situation in a useful way.
  d. All of the above

_____ **18.** Stress is the body's response to
  a. new or unpleasant situations.
  b. love and hate.
  c. negative self-talk.
  d. None of the above

_____ **19.** Devaluation is a defense mechanism in which a person
  a. uses positive self-talk to feel better.
  b. thinks negatively about a situation in order to find a healthy solution to a problem.
  c. thinks positively about a negative situation.
  d. thinks negatively about another person in order to ignore a negative situation.

_____ **20.** A trigger is
  a. a person, situation, or event that influences your emotions.
  b. someone that helps you out of a bad situation.
  c. something that makes you think.
  d. All of the above

Lesson: Mental Illness

21. Stressful life events may cause changes in the _____ which could lead to mental illness.

22. A _____ is a disorder that affects a person's thoughts, emotions, and behaviors.

23. Talking about thoughts and changing behaviors is called

_____.

24. A mental illness that can affect a person's mood is called a

_____.

25. A disorder that makes a person sad and hopeless for a long time is called

_____.

| Concept Review *continued*

26. The most dangerous part of depression is the possibility of

_____.

27. A mood disorder in which a person has depression and mania is called

_____.

28. Another name for bipolar mood disorder is _____.

29. _____ is an excited mood that is associated with

excessive energy or irritation.

30. To _____ is to see things or hear things that don't exist.

31. A mental illness that affects thoughts and behaviors more than it affects

moods is called _____.

32. Disorders that cause nervousness, worry, or panic are called

_____ disorders.

33. When a person feels anxiety about thoughts that he or she has over and over

again, it may be a sign of _____.

Lesson: Getting Help

34. List three sources of help for emotional problems.

_____

_____

_____

35. Explain when to find help for others who have emotional problems.

_____

_____

_____

36. Describe how to know when you need help for an emotional problem.

_____

_____

_____

_____

Activity

Health Inventory

Mental and Emotional Health

Read each of the following statements. Think about how well it describes your behavior. Write *always, sometimes,* or *never* in the space to the left of each statement.

_____ **1.** If I were feeling confused about a situation, I would decide to talk to my parents or friends about my emotions.

_____ **2.** I would not skip class or school if I were feeling sad.

_____ **3.** I make my decisions about people based on experiences, rather than prejudice.

_____ **4.** I take responsibility for myself when I get a poor grade on a test rather than getting angry with my teacher.

_____ **5.** I listen closely when other people talk about their thoughts or emotions.

_____ **6.** I know how to cope with unpleasant emotions.

_____ **7.** I know where I could get help for myself or for a friend with emotional problems.

_____ **8.** I know what my triggers are and how to avoid situations that trigger unpleasant emotions.

Score yourself for this inventory. Give yourself 5 points for each *always,* 3 points for each *sometimes,* and 0 points for each *never.* Write your score here _____.

36–40: Excellent—You are good at dealing with emotions.
32–35: Good—You are able to maintain emotional health, but you could work a bit harder to deal with your emotions sometimes.
28–31: Fair—You should practice strategies for dealing with your emotions.
Less than 28: You need to learn more about dealing with emotions. You may want to talk it over with a trusted adult.

Name _____ Class _____ Date _____

Health Behavior Contract

Mental and Emotional Health

My Goals: I, _____, will accomplish one or more of the following goals:

I will practice good communication skills.

I will use positive self-talk to overcome negative thinking.

I will find an activity that triggers pleasant emotions.

Other: _____

_____

My Reasons: By improving my ability to communicate, to think through emotional problems, and to trigger pleasant emotions, I will improve my mental and emotional health.

Other: _____

_____

My Values: Personal values that will help me meet my goals are

_____

_____

_____

My Plan: The actions I will take to meet my goals are

_____

_____

_____

Evaluation: I will use my Health Journal to keep a log of actions I took to fulfill this contract. After 1 month, I will evaluate my goals. I will adjust my plan if my goals are not being met. If my goals are being met, I will consider setting additional goals.

Signed _____

Date _____

Activity

Life Skills: Communicating Effectively

Lesson: Expressing Emotions
OPENING UP TO TO A FRIEND
Read the following situation. Then, answer the questions.

Your friend Ruthann has been unusually preoccupied lately. She can't even seem to carry on a conversation without getting up and leaving, or staring into space. Whenever anyone has tried to talk with her, she has changed the subject of the conversation. You used to tell her all of your problems, but now when talk to her, she doesn't listen to you. Ruthann's behavior concerns you and you've decided to ask her if she is OK. You are not sure how to approach her in a way that will convince her to confide in you. You are concerned that if she hasn't talked about her problems thus far, she will not want to do it now.

1. What seems to be wrong with Ruthann?

_____

_____

_____

2. How could you communicate your concerns to Ruthann?

_____

_____

_____

3. Where could you suggest Ruthann go for support and to get help with her problem?

_____

_____

_____

4. If Ruthann will not get help on her own, to whom could you go with your concerns?

_____

_____

_____

Activity

Life Skills: Coping

Lesson: Getting Help
DEALING WITH STRESS

Gregg is feeling very stressed over the amount of work he has in his life. He has extra projects to complete for his enriched language class at school, his soccer coach expects him to attend two more practice sessions a week, he has a piano recital coming up in a week, and his grandfather is coming for a visit. He doesn't want to share his feelings with his parents because he thinks that's what little kids do. He feels he has lost control of his life. Gregg is finding it hard to talk to his friends about his stress, and he wishes he could talk to an impartial listener about his problems. What should Gregg do?

1. Where should Gregg go to get help with his problem?

_____

_____

2. Who can Gregg seek who will be impartial in his or her judgment of Gregg's problems?

_____

_____

3. Would Gregg need to see a psychiatrist or a therapist? Which one would be more effective and why?

_____

_____

_____

4. List some healthy ways to cope with stress.

_____

_____

_____

_____

_____

Skills Worksheet

Concept Review

Lesson: Stress Is Only Natural

In the blanks provided, fill in the letters of the term or phrase being described.

1. Anything that triggers a stress response. _ _ R _ _ _ _ _ R

2. It can help you meet your goals. _ O _ _ _ I _ _ S _ _ _ _ S

3. It can leave you feeling tired and depressed. _ _ S _ _ E _ _

4. Your body's natural response to threatening situations. _ T _ _ S _

In the blanks provided, write _P_ next to examples of positive (good) stress and _D_ next to examples of distress (bad stress).

_____ **5.** fighting with your best friend

_____ **6.** missing your bus

_____ **7.** celebrating a special birthday

_____ **8.** winning a chess tournament

_____ **9.** getting braces

_____ **10.** making the cheerleading squad

11. In the stress inventory, the stressor "Being rejected for an extracurricular activity" has a higher stress rating than "Beginning middle school." Do you agree? Explain your answer.

_____

_____

_____

_____

12. Give one example of positive stress you can identify in your life and one example of distress in your life.

Positive stress: _____

Distress: _____

13. You must be careful to protect your _____ if you experience a high level of stress over a long period of time.

Concept Review *continued*

14. Provide one example of a warning sign of stress.

_____

_____

_____

_____

_____

_____

Lesson: The Effects of Stress

_____**15.** Which of the following is NOT a physical reaction to stress?

    a. More blood goes to the brain.

    b. The heart beats faster and harder.

    c. The throat becomes sore.

    d. Breathing speeds up.

16. Give three examples of each of the following effects of stress.

Emotional effects of stress

_____

_____

Mental effects of stress

_____

_____

_____

17. Imagine that you're camping in the woods and suddenly a black bear appears outside your tent. Use the words: *stress response*, *epinephrine*, and *energy boost* to describe what would be happening to you and what you would do.

_____

_____

_____

_____

| Concept Review *continued*

18. A stress response is a set of _____ changes that prepare

your body to act in response to a _____.

19. Physical or mental exhaustion, a common effect of long-term stress, is called

_____.

20. Give two examples of the physical effects of fatigue.

_____

_____

21. What type of stress are you experiencing when you're always angry and your family and friends don't want to be around?

_____

_____

Lesson: Defense Mechanisms

Match each definitions with the correct term. Write the letter in the space provided.

_____ **22.** lasting for a brief time

_____ **23.** using your imagination to escape an unpleasant situation

_____ **24.** refusing to accept reality

_____ **25.** protecting yourself from being hurt emotionally

_____ **26.** contending with difficulties, especially successfully

_____ **27.** responding involuntarily (with little or no external control)

_____ **28.** blocking out unpleasant thoughts or memories

a. coping

b. defense mechanism

c. short-term

d. repression

e. daydreaming

f. automatic

g. denial

| Concept Review continued

Fill in the blanks using the following terms: *recognize, automatic, problem, distress, cope, self-esteem,* **and** *manage.*

29. Defense mechanisms can _____ your distress, but they

don't fix the real _____.

30. It's important to _____ a defense mechanism and to

analyze why you are finding it necessary to use one.

31. Defense mechanisms are ways you have learned to deal quickly with

_____.

32. Defense mechanisms are short-term, unconscious, and

_____ ways to _____ with distress.

33. Your defense mechanisms help you maintain your _____.

34. Give two examples of common defense mechanisms.

_____

_____

Lesson: Managing Distress

Complete the following paragraph using the following words: *physically, distress, unpleasant, frustration, mentally, threatening, heart pounding,* **and** *emotionally.*

A major stressor appears. You interpret it as **35.** _____ or

36. _____. You respond **37.** _____,

38. _____, and **39.** _____, and begin

to show signs of **40.** _____, such as

41. _____ and **42.** _____,

In the blanks provided, fill in the letters of the term or phrase being described.

43. The ability to handle stress in healthy ways is __ __ R __ __ __ __

__ A __ A __ __ __ __ __ T.

44. Three ways to manage stress are __ __ L __ __ __ __ I __ __,

R __ __ __ __ __ __ T __ __ __, and __ E __ R __ __ __ __ __.

| **Concept Review** *continued* |

45. Place the following list of warning signs of distress under the appropriate heading: *mood swings, teeth grinding, fatigue, nightmares, frustration, headaches, depression,* and *heart pounding.*

Warning Signs of Distress	
Physical Signs	**Emotional and Mental Signs**

46. Explain how you could use relaxation to manage the stress of worrying about a fight you had with your friend.

_____

_____

_____

_____

47. Explain how you could use redirection to manage the stress of achieving an important personal goal.

_____

_____

_____

_____

48. Imagine that you are an expert at stress management and have been asked to counsel your classmates on how to avoid distress. What is the most important tip you would give them? Why is your tip important?

_____

_____

_____

_____

_____

Activity

Health Inventory

Managing Stress

**Read each statement below. Decide how it describes your feelings about stress.
Write *always*, *sometimes*, or *never* in the space to the left of each statement.**

_____ 1. I force myself to react the same way my friends do to stressors.

_____ 2. I expect to have control over all of my stressors.

_____ 3. I sleep a lot more than usual if I'm coping well with distress.

_____ 4. I avoid stress, even if it could be fun and exciting.

_____ 5. If I'm already feeling distressed, I think it doesn't matter much if a few more stressors are added to my stress inventory.

_____ 6. I'm too young to worry about the long-term effects of stress.

_____ 7. When I'm under stress, my senses are sharpened and I do better on assignments and tests.

_____ 8. I rely on defense mechanisms as my number one way to manage stress.

_____ 9. I find that the warning signs of stress go away if I ignore them.

_____ 10. I'm so busy, I don't have the time to think about the stress I'm feeling.

**Score yourself: Give yourself 4 points for each *never* answer, 2 points for each
sometimes answer, and 0 points for each *always* answer.
Write your score here _____.**

35–40: Excellent—You are a good stress manager.
25–34: Good—You are well on your way to being a part of the management team.
15–24: Fair—You need some more work before you can expect a promotion.
Fewer than 15: You need to request additional training in stress management.

Name _____ Class _____ Date _____

Health Behavior Contract

Managing Stress

My Goals: I, _____, will accomplish one or more of the following goals:

I will identify three trusted adults whom I could tell about a stressor that is worrying me.

I will make a plan to manage one of my stressors.

I will practice using my refusal skills to relieve the stress from one of my stressors.

Other: _____
_____

My Reasons: By managing my stress, I will reduce the long-term effects that stress can have on me. I can also develop stress management skills, learn better communication skills, and help keep myself healthy.

Other: _____
_____

My Values: Personal values that will help me meet my goals are

_____

_____

_____

My Plan: The actions I will take to meet my goals are

_____

_____

_____

Evaluation: I will use my Health Journal to keep a log of actions I took to fulfill this contract. After 1 month, I will evaluate my goals. I will adjust my plan if my goals are not being met. If my goals are being met, I will consider setting additional goals.

Signed _____

Date _____

Name _____ Class _____ Date _____

Life Skills: Coping

Lesson: The Effects of Stress
RESPONDING TO STRESSORS

Label the figure provided below with the specific physical reactions the stress response produces. Then, answer the questions.

1. Explain how the physical changes produced by a stress response get your body ready for "fight or flight."

_____

_____

_____

2. Most of the stress response changes will go away when the stressor is gone, but what happens if the stressor is not eliminated?

_____

_____

_____

Activity

Life Skills: Communicating Effectively

Lesson: Managing Distress
CREATING AN EXERCISE PACKAGE
Read the following situation, and answer the questions that follow.

Imagine you are the director of advertising for a company that provides stress management products. You're excited because you're about to launch a new exercise package to help people manage their stress by planning their physical exercise activities. The package is going to include a calendar, a stress management checklist, a list of distress management tips, and a video of exercises.

1. What is one thing you would include on the stress management checklist?

_____

_____

2. What are two things you would include on the list of distress management tips?

_____

_____

_____

3. Write a 2-sentence introduction for the videotape. Be sure to highlight why physical activity is important in managing stress.

_____

_____

_____

_____

4. If you had to choose someone who would present a positive image for your new product to star in the videotape, who would it be? Please explain.

_____

_____

_____

_____

Skills Worksheet

Concept Review

Lesson: Building Relationships

Match each definition with the correct term. Write the correct letter in the space provided.

_____ **1.** the way you choose to act or respond

_____ **2.** an emotional or social connection between two or more people

_____ **3.** doing your part, keeping promises, and accepting the consequences of your actions

_____ **4.** a way of communicating by using facial expressions, the way you hold your hands, and the way you stand

a. relationship

b. personal responsibility

c. body language

d. behavior

Write the letter of the correct answer in the space provided.

_____ **5.** When people in relationships are good to each other, they can help keep each other
  a. awake and alert.
  b. safe and healthy.
  c. in danger.
  d. None of the above

_____ **6.** When you are responsible, you correct your mistakes and
  a. learn from them.
  b. help others make the same mistakes you did.
  c. make new mistakes.
  d. never make the same mistake again.

_____ **7.** Being responsible in a relationship is
  a. taking control of both your life and someone else's life.
  b. thinking first about yourself.
  c. allowing the other person in the relationship to have all the control.
  d. like being on a team.

_____ **8.** Taking care of small problems that you see around the house shows that you care about
  a. only small problems.
  b. only your own things.
  c. your role in your family.
  d. your friends.

| Concept Review *continued*

9. Using good _____ skills helps people share thoughts and feelings.

10. Name four good listening skills.

_____

_____

_____

_____

11. Sending the same message clearly through both your

_____ and your _____ helps get

your message across.

12. Acting on your thoughts and feelings in a way that respects the thoughts and

feelings of others is being _____.

Lesson: Family Relationships

Match each definition with the correct term. Write the correct letter in the space provided.

_____**13.** two families that come together into one new family

_____**14.** the failure of a parent or responsible adult to provide for a child's basic needs, such as food, clothing, and shelter

_____**15.** a family that provides the things people need in order to live and grow

_____**16.** grandparents, aunts, uncles, and cousins

_____**17.** treating someone in a harmful or offensive way

a. nurturing family

b. neglect

c. abuse

d. blended family

e. extended family

Write the letter of the correct answer in the space provided.

_____**18.** Which of the following is NOT a way to show respect for your family?
  a. follow family rules
  b. complain when things don't go your way
  c. keep your word
  d. discuss disagreements respectfully

19. For your family to _____ smoothly, everyone must do his or her part.

20. Name four things nurturing families provide for one another.

_____

_____

_____

_____

21. Problems such as arguments between brothers and sisters can usually be

solved if the people involved _____ to each other,

_____ together, and look for a solution that works for

everyone.

22. If you know of anyone being abused or neglected, help that person by

_____ the problem as soon as you can.

Lesson: Healthy Communities

Write the letter of the correct answer in the space provided.

_____**23.** Which of the following is NOT an example of a community?
  a. a neighborhood
  b. a school
  c. a team
  d. a karate teacher

_____**24.** Which of the following is NOT a way for you to help keep your community healthy?
  a. demand that you get your way
  b. obey rules and laws
  c. practice tolerance
  d. take part in community activities

25. A community is made up of people who have a common background or

location or who share similar interests, _____, or goals.

26. What is tolerance?

_____

_____

27. By respecting differences in each other, people in a community can

_____ from each other.

Lesson: Building Friendships

Write the letter of the correct answer in the space provided.

_____**28.** Which of the following is NOT a healthy way to support your friends?
    a. cheering for them at a game or performance
    b. asking them to lie for you
    c. helping them with a project or chores
    d. studying or exercising together

_____**29.** Which of the following is NOT a healthy way to show affection?
    a. saying kind words
    b. offering a smile or laugh
    c. mocking someone's mistakes
    d. patting someone on the back

30. What is a friendship?

_____

_____

_____

31. Friends help support your _____ and help you do your
best work in school.

32. Influencing friends to make good decisions is _____.

33. Healthy relationships are _____ when people
show affection.

34. List three ways to know if a relationship is unhealthy.

_____

_____

_____

| Concept Review *continued*

35. If you are in an unhealthy relationship, first talk to your

_____ about resolving it.

Lesson: Practicing Abstinence

_____**36.** Which of the following is NOT a benefit of sexual abstinence?
    a. complicating your life
    b. avoiding pregnancy with 100 percent certainty
    c. avoiding exposure to disease
    d. avoiding emotional scars from being sexually active

37. What is sexual abstinence?

_____

_____

_____

38. Maintaining abstinence in a relationship shows one of the highest levels of

_____ and love for someone.

39. Good friends don't _____ you to change your values or
risk your health.

40. Name two risks of becoming sexually active.

_____

_____

Name _____ Class _____ Date _____

Health Inventory

Encouraging Healthy Relationships

Read each statement below. Decide whether it describes how you treat your family. Write *always*, *sometimes*, or *never* in the space to the left of each statement.

_____ **1.** I love and accept every member of my family.

_____ **2.** I follow family rules.

_____ **3.** I practice the values my family taught me.

_____ **4.** I keep my word.

_____ **5.** I discuss disagreements respectfully.

_____ **6.** I treat my family members' property as I would treat my own.

_____ **7.** I treat my family members' rooms as I would want mine treated.

_____ **8.** I respect other family members' privacy.

_____ **9.** I listen carefully when a family member speaks to me.

_____ **10.** I respond politely when a family member asks me a question.

Score yourself: Give yourself 3 points for each *always* answer, 1 point for each *sometimes*, and 0 for each *never*. Write your score here _____ .

28–30: Excellent—You always practice healthy family relationships.
22–27: Good—You often practice healthy family relationship skills.
11–21: Fair—You can improve on your family relationships.
0–10: You need to work on your family relationship skills.

Activity

Health Behavior Contract

Encouraging Healthy Relationships

My Goals: I, _____, will accomplish one or more of the following goals:

I will identify three trusted adults with whom I could talk about a serious problem.

I will show support to a friend or family member.

I will use my refusal skills when someone tries to pressure me into doing something that I do not want to do.

Other: _____

_____

My Reasons: By talking to an adult about a problem, I can help keep myself safe and healthy. By supporting my family and friends, I will learn better communication skills and how to improve my relationships with them. I will also develop assertive behavior when I use refusal skills.

Other: _____

_____

My Values: Personal values that will help me meet my goals are

_____

_____

_____

My Plan: The actions I will take to meet my goals are

_____

_____

_____

Evaluation: I will use my Health Journal to keep a log of actions I took to fulfill this contract. After 1 month, I will evaluate my goals. I will adjust my plan if my goals are not being met. If my goals are being met, I will consider setting additional goals.

Signed _____

Date _____

Activity

Life Skills: Communicating Effectively

Lesson: Building Relationships
COMMUNICATING WITH FRIENDS

Conflict with friends can be frustrating. Knowing when a relationship is unhealthy and how to communicate this is even more difficult. Consider the following situation.

Kevin and Chad have been friends since kindergarten, but they've been hanging out less and less since Kevin started playing soccer. Kevin tried to convince Chad to join the soccer team, but Chad refused. He said he had better things to do than run around a field all day chasing a ball. These remarks hurt Kevin's feelings but he put his feelings aside. Then, last week Chad asked Kevin to skip his soccer match so they could go to a movie together. When Kevin said no, Chad got angry. "Some friend you are," he said.

Answer the following questions:

1. Do you think Kevin and Chad have a healthy relationship? Explain.

_____

_____

_____

2. What specific behaviors lead you to think this?

_____

_____

_____

3. How could Kevin communicate his feeling to Chad?

_____

_____

_____

4. What could Chad do to show Kevin he was listening to him? How could Chad communicate his frustration to Kevin without becoming angry?

_____

_____

_____

Activity

Life Skills: Setting Goals

Lesson: Healthy Communities
GOALS FOR A HEALTHY COMMUNITY

A community is made up of people who have a common background or location or who share similar interests, beliefs, or goals. Neighborhoods, schools, and teams are examples of communities. To help keep a community healthy, the members

- obey rules and laws
- practice tolerance
- take part in community activities
- respectfully point out problems
- work with others to find solutions to community problems

Choose one of the communities of which you are a member. Then choose one of the objectives from above as a long-term goal to help keep your community healthy. List four to five short-term goals or steps you can take NOW to help you reach your long-term goal. Use the space below to outline your plan.

Skills Worksheet

Concept Review

Lesson: What Is Conflict?

1. What is a clash of of ideas or interests called?

_____

_____

2. Give three examples of the signs that a conflict is happening or is about to happen.

_____

_____

_____

3. Give three examples of where and with whom conflict typically happens.

_____

_____

_____

4. What is bullying? Give an example of behavior that is bullying.

_____

_____

_____

_____

5. Describe a situation in which conflict might arise when you are having fun with a friend.

_____

_____

_____

_____

_____

_____

Label each of the following conflicts with its cause: *resources, values and expectations,* **or** *emotions.*

_____ **6.** A brother and sister want to watch different shows that are on television at the same time.

_____ **7.** Lisa feels hurt because she wasn't invited to a friend's birthday party.

_____ **8.** Carl's parents want him to clean up the dinner dishes and read a bedtime story to his younger sister before he plays a video game.

Lesson: Communicating During Conflicts

9. Why is using good communication helpful during a conflict?

_____

_____

10. Describe what *choosing the right words* in a conflict means.

_____

_____

_____

11. List three good listening skills.

_____

_____

_____

12. What is negotiation, and what is necessary for it to work?

_____

_____

_____

13. What is the difference between compromise and collaboration?

_____

_____

▌Concept Review *continued*

In the following puzzle, circle the examples of body language and listening skills and write them under the correct heading. Words can appear horizontally, vertically, or diagonally. (Word list: *angry look, eye contact, finger pointing, fist shaking, folded arms, frown, not interrupting, paying attention, relaxed body, repeating what is said,* and *standing close.*)

Facial Expressions   Gestures

14. _____   19. _____

15. _____   20. _____

Posture   Listening Skills

16. _____   21. _____

17. _____   22. _____

18. _____   23. _____

                                                                24. _____

```
a e f n c j z e o t l c a l g h i l n
f y v k f u z m b f c c r t v y h f f
r e p e a t i n g w h a t i s s a i d
o c u f e x i o n m l y v v m m n z v
w o t o i g t i i v v m c u r b g z j
n n h i b n e t t n e y l v a i r e z
w t h u l i g n p i j s g o d i y r g
k a y z k k p e u b b t v w e a l q j
i c u z f a l t r e l a x e d b o d y
d t a h s h z t r p c n u y l l o p g
m a o w s s w a e h o d x t o k k p k
u f s h h t a g t p g i h z f e k u u
g e t t k s o n n l j n n t m t q u k
d y u r h i p i i v u g t t l k m v b
q s b e q f v y t m u c p i i h n v h
k u w f w l n a o v f l y o j n u w m
k s b f s f e p n p z o l n u r g v l
a f n q g r c d h l c s m l f e h o q
v a j p s w d a u a e e p x v h b k i
```

Name _____ Class _____ Date _____

Lesson: Getting Help for Conflicts

25. Why is it helpful to know that a conflict is out of control?

_____

_____

26. What are five signs that a conflict is out of control?

_____

_____

_____

_____

27. Explain what a mediator is and how mediation can help solve out-of-control conflicts.

_____

_____

_____

_____

28. What are seven things that training teaches a mediator to do?

_____

_____

_____

_____

_____

_____

| Concept Review *continued*

Lesson: Violence: When Conflict Becomes Dangerous

29. What is violence?

_____

_____

30. Explain how bad communication can cause a conflict to become violent.

_____

_____

31. What can you accomplish by walking away from a conflict that has signs of becoming violent?

_____

_____

32. Give three examples of signs that a conflict might become violent.

_____

_____

_____

33. What is a possible consequence of not reporting a threat?

_____

_____

_____

34. Give two examples of aggression.

_____

_____

35. Explain the difference between violence, aggression, and threats.

_____

_____

_____

_____

Concept Review *continued*

Lesson: Preventing Violence

36. What can happen if anger is not expressed in a healthy way?

_____

_____

37. Give one example of each of the five strategies to stop anger from turning to violence.

_____

_____

_____

_____

38. What are five things that you can do to lower your risk of becoming a victim of violence?

_____

_____

_____

39. What behaviors increase the chance that a person will become violent in a conflict?

_____

_____

Name _____ Class _____ Date _____

Activity

Health Inventory

Conflict and Violence

Read the statements below. Check the box that best describes your behavior in a conflict.

always	some-times	never	
❑	❑	❑	**1.** I watch out for the signs that conflict is happening.
❑	❑	❑	**2.** I choose my words carefully and avoid words that are hurtful.
❑	❑	❑	**3.** I express my feelings and expectations accurately.
❑	❑	❑	**4.** I keep a calm expression on my face.
❑	❑	❑	**5.** I avoid making threatening gestures.
❑	❑	❑	**6.** I avoid using conflicting types of body language.
❑	❑	❑	**7.** I make eye contact with the person speaking.
❑	❑	❑	**8.** I avoid becoming distracted by things going on around me.
❑	❑	❑	**9.** I repeat what someone who is speaking said if I'm not sure I understood it.
❑	❑	❑	**10.** I avoid interrupting someone who is speaking.
❑	❑	❑	**11.** I am willing to discuss my feelings openly and honestly.
❑	❑	❑	**12.** I am willing to make sacrifices to reach a solution.
❑	❑	❑	**13.** I watch out for the signs that a conflict is out of control.
❑	❑	❑	**14.** I take a break if I am in a conflict that is out of control.
❑	❑	❑	**15.** I would use a mediator to solve an out-of-control conflict.
❑	❑	❑	**16.** I watch out for the signs that a conflict may become violent.
❑	❑	❑	**17.** I report any aggression or threats that I see or hear.
❑	❑	❑	**18.** I practice strategies to control anger.
❑	❑	❑	**19.** I protect myself from becoming a victim of violence.

Score yourself: Give yourself 3 points for each *always* answer, 1 point for each *sometimes*, and 0 points for each *never*. Write your score here_____.

46–57: Excellent—You always handle conflict effectively.
31–45: Good—You often handle conflict effectively.
16–30: Fair—You can do better at handling conflict effectively.
Less than 16: You need to work on handling conflict effectively.

Name _____ Class _____ Date _____

Health Behavior Contract

Conflict and Violence

My Goals: I, _____, will accomplish one or more of the following goals:

I will use good communication skills to avoid conflicts.

I will control my anger.

I will avoid situations that could become violent.

Other: _____

_____

My Reasons: By expressing myself clearly and calmly, using good body language, and listening well, I will increase my chances of avoiding conflicts. By controlling my anger and by avoiding dangerous situations, I can prevent violence.

Other: _____

_____

My Values: Personal values that will help me meet my goals are

_____

_____

_____

My Plan: The actions I will take to meet my goals are

_____

_____

_____

Evaluation: I will use my Health Journal to keep a log of actions I took to fulfill this contract. After 1 month, I will evaluate my goals. I will adjust my plan if my goals are not being met. If my goals are being met, I will consider setting additional goals.

Signed _____

Date _____

Name _____ Class _____ Date _____

Activity

Life Skills: Communicating Effectively

Lesson: Communicating During Conflicts
DISCUSSION VERSUS ARGUMENT IN A CONFLICT

Takesha and her sister Arletta both need to use the family's computer to do their homework and each wants to use it right away so there will be time to watch their favorite television show after dinner. Both girls feel angry.

Situation A Takesha is speaking very loudly and harshly as she insists that she should be first to use the computer. Arletta interrupts her constantly. The girls start calling each other names and hurling insults. They make accusations about each other that are exaggerated. Takesha and Arletta both want to win their argument.

Situation B Takesha and Arletta each are explaining why she should be the first to use the computer. They both have a friendly, respectful attitude and they choose their words exactly and carefully. They speak calmly. Both listen attentively and quietly. Takesha and Arletta both want their discussion to result in a solution to their conflict.

Write what you think the two sisters would say in each situation. Describe the feelings of the participants, the goal of the participants, and the possible outcome of each situation.

   1. Situation A

_____

_____

_____

_____

_____

_____

_____

_____

_____

_____

_____

Life Skills *continued.*

2. Situation B

_____

_____

_____

_____

_____

_____

_____

_____

3. Can you feel angry and still have a productive discussion? Explain.

_____

_____

_____

_____

_____

_____

_____

_____

_____

_____

_____

Activity

Life Skills: Coping

Lesson: Violence: When Conflict Becomes Dangerous
RECOGNIZING AND HANDLING AGGRESSION AND THREATS

Conflicts that are heading toward violence can be upsetting, but there are appropriate ways to respond. Making responsible choices lessens the feelings of fear that you might experience if you see signs that a violent conflict is about to happen. Consider the following situation.

Two girls are standing near Andy's locker as he walks toward it. As Andy gets closer to the girls, he sees that one of them has clenched her jaw and is talking through tightened lips. Andy overhears her say, "We're going to give them what they deserve for treating us this way." The other girl notices Andy approaching, hushes her friend, and then turns toward Andy. She smiles and winks and then says in a light, laughing tone to Andy, "Don't look so worried. You know we're just kidding around."

1. Did Andy hear a threat? Explain.

_____

_____

_____

_____

2. Describe how Andy might have felt after hearing what the girls said.

_____

_____

_____

_____

_____

_____

_____

_____

3. What should Andy do in response to what he heard?

_____

_____

_____

_____

4. Give examples of people to whom Andy might report what he heard.

_____

_____

_____

_____

5. Compare and contrast how Andy might feel if he reports the threat and how he might feel if he does not report the threat and a violent situation occurs later.

_____

_____

_____

_____

_____

_____

_____

_____

_____

Skills Worksheet

Concept Review

Lesson: Tobacco: Dangerous from the Start

In the blanks provided, write C beside the chemicals that are produced when tobacco products are burned and A beside the substances that are additives to tobacco products.

_____ **1.** carbon monoxide

_____ **2.** ammonia

_____ **3.** tar

_____ **4.** benzene

_____ **5.** nicotine

6. What makes secondhand smoke, or environmental tobacco smoke, harmful to the health of nonsmokers?

_____

_____

7. Describe one smokeless tobacco product, and explain how it affects your health.

_____

_____

Lesson: Tobacco Products, Disease, and Death

Use the terms from the following list to complete the sentences below. Each term may be used only once. One term will not be used.

chronic bronchitis	oral cancer	lung cancer	birth defects
cardiovascular disease	stroke	nicotine	

8. Smokers are at far greater risk of coronary artery disease, and other types of

_____ than nonsmokers are.

9. Smokers often cough a lot and have _____ because their airways are constantly irritated by cigarette smoke.

10. Smoking has harmful effects on the body's circulatory system and may, at some point, cut off the blood flow to the brain causing a

_____ .

Concept Review *continued*

11. Smokers and users of smokeless tobacco often get sores inside their mouth, and with continued exposure to tobacco, may develop into

_____.

12. The incidence of _____, in which cells in the lungs grow uncontrollably, is far greater among smokers than nonsmokers.

13. A pregnant woman who smokes runs the risk of having a low-birthweight

baby or a baby who has _____.

Lesson: Social and Emotional Effects of Tobacco

In the blanks provided, write *B* for those actions that involve breaking the law and write *S* for those actions that cause other kinds of social strain.

_____14. lying about your age to buy cigarettes.

_____15. smoking at a friend's house when the parents are not home

_____16. smoking in an airplane

_____17. smoking at a school event

_____18. smoking at a smoke-free restaurant

_____19. buying cigarettes for young children

_____20. smoking in the schoolyard even though it's against the law

Lesson: Forming a Tobacco Addiction

In the blanks provided, fill in the letters of the term or phrase being described.

21. a condition in which a person can no longer control his or her need for a substance
    A __ __ I __ __ __ __ N

22. a condition in which a person needs more of a drug to get the same effect
    T __ __ E __ __ __ __ E

23. how the body responds when a dependent person stops using a drug
    W __ __ __ __ R __ __ __ __

24. What does having a dependence on nicotine mean?

_____

_____

25. What role do the nicotine receptors in the brain play in a smoker's developing an addiction to tobacco products?

_____

_____

26. How does tolerance to nicotine lead to dependence on tobacco products?

_____

_____

27. Describe three withdrawal effects experienced by smokers when they are deprived of cigarettes for a period of time.

_____

_____

Lesson: Why People Use Tobacco

Write the letter of the correct answer in the space provided.

_____ **28.** Peer pressure involves which of the following?
   a. advice from teachers
   b. strong influence from classmates
   c. advertising that makes something appear glamorous
   d. exposure to environmental tobacco smoke

_____ **29.** Teenagers often may start to smoke cigarettes because they want to
   a. have a habit.
   b. do what their parents do.
   c. break the law.
   d. engage in an adult activity.

_____ **30.** Studies have shown that most teenage smokers
   a. want to quit smoking.
   b. can afford to buy cigarettes.
   c. rarely watch ads on TV.
   d. have few friends who smoke.

_____ **31.** Aiming ads at a particular group of people is called
   a. focus grouping.
   b. creating peer pressure.
   c. targeted advertising.
   d. habit forming.

Name _____ Class _____ Date _____

_____**32.** Advertising attracts teenagers to smoking by
    a. pointing out that smoking is not harmful to young people.
    b. showing smoking's health effects on adults.
    c. showing attractive teens smoking and having fun.
    d. ignoring the laws against smoking.

_____**33.** In which of the following places is cigarette advertising always allowed?
    a. on roadside billboards
    b. on television
    c. on the radio
    d. None of the above

Lesson: Quitting

34. Why is it difficult to quit smoking?

_____

_____

35. What are three unpleasant symptoms a person who is trying to quit smoking cigarettes may experience?

_____

_____

_____

36. What are three strategies a smoker can use to quit smoking cigarettes?

_____

_____

_____

37. What is nicotine replacement therapy, and how does it help a person quit using tobacco?

_____

_____

_____

Name _____ Class _____ Date _____

For each place listed below, write an *S* if smoking is allowed there or an *N* if smoking is not allowed.

_____ **38.** at a smoker's house

_____ **39.** at the movies

_____ **40.** at a school event

_____ **41.** in an airplane

_____ **42.** on a train

_____ **43.** on the street

_____ **44.** in an office

_____ **45.** on a bus

_____ **46.** in a store

_____ **47.** at the shopping mall

Lesson: Choosing Not to Use Tobacco

Complete each sentence below.

48. Refusing to smoke a cigarette can be stressful when

_____

_____

49. An example of positive peer pressure is

_____

_____

50. It is better for you if you have friends who don't smoke because

_____

_____

51. One good reason to refuse tobacco is because the nicotine in tobacco is very

_____ and may become habit forming.

52. Using tobacco may negatively affect your social life because it makes your

breath, your skin, and your hair _____ bad.

| Concept Review *continued*

53. The very high taxes many states have put on cigarettes makes them very

_____, so buying them takes money away from more

important things.

On lines below, write one way you can refuse to smoke a cigarette in each scenario.

54. "Try it, just one won't hurt!"

_____

_____

55. "Only creeps won't smoke."

_____

_____

56. "Come on, it's cool!"

_____

_____

57. "You can hang out with us only if you smoke a cigarette."

_____

_____

58. "What's the matter, are you scared?"

_____

_____

Name _____ Class _____ Date _____

Health Inventory

Teens and Tobacco

Use the following questions to help you evaluate the health risks that tobacco and tobacco products pose to your health. Read each item, and check the box that represents your answer.

yes	no		
❏	❏	**1.** Do you smoke?	35 points
❏	❏	**2.** Do members of your immediate family smoke?	15 points
❏	❏	**3.** Do you have close friends who smoke?	10 points
❏	❏	**4.** Do family members whom you see less than once a week smoke?	8 points
❏	❏	**5.** Do you have acquaintances who smoke?	5 points
❏	❏	**6.** Of the people you admire, do any of them smoke cigarettes or use other tobacco products?	5 points
❏	❏	**7.** Does cigarette smoking seem glamorous to you?	6 points
❏	❏	**8.** Do you feel nervous when you are not holding something in your hands?	5 points
❏	❏	**9.** Do you find yourself sitting in a smoke-filled room at least once a week?	3 points
❏	❏	**10.** Do you find yourself sitting in a smoke-filled room at least once a day?	8 points

Add up the points for all of the questions to which you answered yes. Look at the scale to see how much of a problem smoking and tobacco products pose to your health.

SCALE	
70 to 100 points	Tobacco products are a big part of your life and probably pose a significant risk to your health.
50 to 69 points	Tobacco products could become a big part of your life and pose a significant risk to your health.
30 to 49 points	Tobacco products could become part of your life and pose some risk to your health.
10 to 29 points	Tobacco products are unlikely to become a big part of your life or pose a significant risk to your health.
Under 10 points	At this point in your life, your health risks from tobacco products are very low.

Name _____ Class _____ Date _____

Health Behavior Contract

Teens and Tobacco

My Goals: I, _____, will accomplish one or more of the following goals:

I will not use tobacco products.

I will help a friend who is being pressured to try tobacco products.

I will encourage friends or family members who smoke to quit smoking.

Other: _____

_____

My Reasons: By refusing to use tobacco products, I will decrease my risk of tobacco-related illnesses. I will also be a positive influence to other people who may be tempted to use tobacco or who are trying to break the habit.

Other: _____

_____

My Values: Personal values that will help me meet my goals are

_____

_____

_____

My Plan: The actions I will take to meet my goals are

_____

_____

_____

Evaluation: I will use my Health Journal to keep a log of actions I took to fulfill this contract. After 1 month, I will evaluate my goals. I will adjust my plan if my goals are not being met. If my goals are being met, I will consider setting additional goals.

Signed _____

Date _____

Activity

Life Skills: Assessing Your Health

Lesson: Tobacco Products, Disease, and Death
HOW ILLNESS AFFECTS YOUR LIFE

Cigarettes harm your health in many different ways. Below are listed some of the ways that tobacco products affect your health. For each item listed, write down how that particular health problem would affect something you like to do in your life. For example, shortness of breath would make it difficult or impossible for you to engage in many sports or even go for long walks.

1. Chronic bronchitis, with coughing

_____

_____

2. Emphysema, with extreme shortness of breath

_____

_____

3. High heart rate and high-blood pressure

_____

_____

4. Mouth sores and oral cancer

_____

_____

5. Frequent colds and flu

_____

_____

6. Bad breath and gum disease

_____

_____

Name _____ Class _____ Date _____

Life Skills: Communicating Effectively

Lesson: Why People Use Tobacco
EVALUATING ADS

Like most people, you have probably seen ads for cigarettes and other tobacco products. These ads make smoking cigarettes look glamorous by showing attractive people in fun situations smoking cigarettes.

Imagine that you have a younger sister or brother who shows an interest in cigarettes because the ads make smoking look exciting. What would you say to discourage him or her from smoking? What would you say to him or her about why people should not trust the image of cigarettes that the ad presents?

On the lines below, write your response to each comment your younger brother or sister might make.

1. "These people look really cool!"

_____

_____

_____

2. "If you smoke, people will like you and you'll be popular."

_____

_____

_____

3. "Cigarettes aren't hurting the people shown in the ad!"

_____

_____

_____

4. Write down three things you would tell your younger brother or sister about cigarette ads and why the ads should not be trusted.

_____

_____

_____

_____

Skills Worksheet

Concept Review

Lesson: Understanding Teens and Alcohol

1. What is a peer?

_____

_____

2. What does it mean if someone is experiencing peer pressure?

_____

_____

_____

3. What are five reasons that teens might drink?

_____

_____

_____

_____

_____

4. How is drinking harmful to teenagers?

_____

_____

_____

_____

Lesson: Alcohol and Your Body

5. What path does alcohol take once it's inside your body?

_____

_____

_____

_____

Concept Review *continued*

6. What are the effects of intoxication?

_____

_____

_____

7. What happens as blood alcohol concentration increases?

_____

_____

_____

8. How is alcohol abuse harmful?

_____

_____

_____

In the blanks provided, fill in the letters of the term or phrase being described.

9. a substance that changes how the mind or body works D __ __ G

10. a drug that slows brain and body functions __ __ P __ __ __ S __ N __

11. the percentage of alcohol in a person's blood __ L __ __ __ __ L __ __ __ L

__ O __ __ __ N __ R __ __ __ O __

12. the physical and mental changes caused by drinking alcohol

__ __ T __ __ __ C __ __ __ __ O __

13. the interval between the moment the brain detects an external stimulus and

the moment there is a response __ E __ __ T __ __ N T __ __ E

14. the failure to drink in moderation or at appropriate times __ __ C __ H __ __ __

__ B U S __

Lesson: Alcohol, You, and Other People

15. How can alcohol lead to a person becoming more violent and more likely to be a victim of violence?

_____

_____

_____

_____

16. Explain why someone who has been drinking doesn't realize that his or her decision-making ability is impaired.

_____

_____

_____

_____

17. Give two examples of how a person's drinking can affect other people.

_____

_____

_____

_____

18. How does alcohol make conflict more difficult to control?

_____

_____

_____

_____

19. What are some of the birth defects associated with fetal alcohol syndrome?

_____

_____

_____

_____

Concept Review *continued*

Lesson: Drunk Driving

20. Describe how alcohol can affect the behavior and the driving skill of a drunk driver.

_____

_____

_____

_____

_____

21. What determines whether someone is legally drunk?

_____

_____

_____

22. What is driving under the influence (DUI)?

_____

_____

_____

_____

23. What can someone do to prevent drunk driving?

_____

_____

_____

_____

_____

_____

| Concept Review *continued*

Lesson: Alcoholism

24. What is alcoholism?

_____

_____

_____

_____

_____

_____

25. How does someone develop alcoholism?

_____

_____

_____

_____

_____

26. How are the family members of someone who has alcoholism affected by this illness?

_____

_____

_____

_____

_____

_____

27. What is recovery, what is required to achieve it, and how is it accomplished?

_____

_____

_____

_____

_____

Name _____ Class _____ Date _____

| Concept Review *continued*

Lesson: Resisting the Pressure to Drink

28. What are examples of internal and external pressures to drink that a teen might experience?

_____

_____

_____

29. How do alcohol advertisements exert pressure on teens to drink?

_____

_____

_____

30. What questions can a teen ask himself or herself to help identify and resist pressures to drink?

_____

_____

_____

Lesson: Alternatives to Alcohol

31. Explain what a hobby is and how it can be a good alternative to drinking. What are other alternatives to drinking?

_____

_____

_____

32. If a teen has a problem with alcohol, whose help should he or she seek?

_____

_____

_____

_____

Name _____ Class _____ Date _____

Health Inventory

Teens and Alcohol

Answer the following questions about the risk factors that influence your choices about using alcohol.

yes	no		
❑	❑	**1.** Have you decided to avoid alcohol at least until you are of legal age?	30 points
❑	❑	**2.** Have you practiced refusal skills on matters of alcohol?	30 points
❑	❑	**3.** Do you avoid situations that might put you at risk because of someone else's drinking?	10 points
❑	❑	**4.** Do you analyze advertisements for alcohol by identifying the real risks of alcohol use?	8 points
❑	❑	**5.** Are you confident of your ability to make decisions for yourself?	5 points
❑	❑	**6.** Do the people you admire drink alcohol?	5 points
❑	❑	**7.** Do you consider the benefits of staying alcohol free?	8 points
❑	❑	**8.** Are you confident of your ability to say no and stick to it even against pressure?	5 points
❑	❑	**9.** Are your risk-taking urges directed to healthy outlets such as sports?	5 points
❑	❑	**10.** Do you have close friends who follow an alcohol-free lifestyle?	10 points

Add up the points for all of the questions to which you answered yes. Write your score here _____.

Use the scale to see how much of a problem alcohol may pose to your health.

SCALE

90–116	You have a strong commitment to staying alcohol free, and you have the personal skills to help you keep your commitment.
60–90	Thinking through your values and goals for your life and making a firm decision about alcohol use will help you make good decisions.
40–60	You have some risk of being vulnerable to pressures to use alcohol.
20–40	You would benefit from learning more about the risks of alcohol use and strengthening your refusal skills.
Less than 20	You need to increase your understanding of what alcohol is and what dangers it poses for you.

Name _____ Class _____ Date _____

Health Behavior Contract

Teens and Alcohol

My Goals: I, _____, will accomplish one or more of the following goals:

I will not drink alcohol.

I will avoid people and places where I may be exposed to pressure to drink alcohol.

I will make a plan for refusing alcohol if it is offered to me.

Other: _____

_____

My Reasons: By refusing to drink alcohol, I will decrease my risk of injury, violence, disease, and behaviors that could lead to death. I will maintain my overall physical, social, and emotional health.

Other: _____

_____

My Values: Personal values that will help me meet my goals are

_____

_____

My Plan: The actions I will take to meet my goals are

_____

_____

_____

Evaluation: I will use my Health Journal to keep a log of actions I took to fulfill this contract. After 1 month, I will evaluate my goals. I will adjust my plan if my goals are not being met. If my goals are being met, I will consider setting additional goals.

Signed _____

Date _____

Name _____ Class _____ Date _____

Life Skills: Evaluating Media Messages

Lesson: Understanding Teens and Alcohol
ADS FOR ALCOHOL

Alcohol advertisements can make drinking seem like a desirable activity. These ads generally do not show the problems involved with drinking

Select a television advertisement for beer, wine, or alcopop, such as hard lemonade or hard cider, that you have seen. Analyze how the ad makes drinking this alcoholic beverage seem attractive. Then, answer the following questions.

1. What is the purpose of the ad?

_____

_____

_____

2. Describe what is happening in the ad.

_____

_____

_____

_____

_____

_____

_____

3. How does the ad make drinking seem appealing?

_____

_____

_____

_____

_____

_____

Copyright © by Holt, Rinehart and Winston. All rights reserved.
Decisions for Health   112   Teens and Alcohol

Name _____ Class _____ Date _____

Life Skills *continued*

4. What are the possible negative aspects of what is happening in the ad?

_____
_____
_____
_____
_____
_____

5. How can you avoid being persuaded to drink by the ad?

_____
_____
_____
_____
_____
_____
_____

6. What is not shown in the ad that should be?

_____
_____
_____
_____
_____
_____
_____

Name _____ Class _____ Date _____

Activity

Life Skills: Coping

Lesson: Alcoholism
DEALING WITH ALCOHOLISM

Your uncle has entered a treatment program for people who have alcoholism. Your cousin Sarah seems angry with and ashamed of her father, and she is avoiding contact with other family members. She has refused several invitations to weekend activities and does not return your phone calls.

Write a letter to Sarah that shows your understanding of her situation but also communicates that alcoholism is an illness. Your letter should stress the importance of your uncle's getting treatment for his illness and his need for your cousin's support.

_____

_____

_____

_____

_____

_____

_____

_____

_____

_____

_____

_____

_____

_____

_____

_____

_____

_____

Name _____ Class _____ Date _____

Concept Review

Lesson: Using Drugs

Match each definition with the correct term. Write the letter in the space provided.

_____ **1.** a coating on capsules that makes them dissolve more slowly to allow the body's cells to absorb the medicine over a long period of time

_____ **2.** a device designed to release certain amounts of a drug stored in air or gas

_____ **3.** medicine in a solid form

_____ **4.** any substance other than food that changes a person's physical or psychological state

_____ **5.** a device that injects a drug into the body

_____ **6.** a patch that sticks to the skin and slowly releases medicine to be absorbed into the bloodstream

_____ **7.** taking medicine through the mouth

_____ **8.** drugs used to numb patients during medical procedures

a. drug
b. orally
c. tablets
d. controlled-release capsules
e. hypodermic needle
f. inhaler
g. anesthetics
h. transdermal patch

Write the letter of the correct answer in the space provided.

_____ **9.** Unlike food, drugs do not provide your body with
  a. flavor.
  b. nutrients.
  c. smoke.
  d. carbon monoxide.

_____ **10.** When smoking a drug, the drug is burned, and the resulting smoke is then
  a. liquidated.
  b. put in a capsule.
  c. inhaled.
  d. exhaled.

| Concept Review *continued*

Lesson: The Use of Drugs as Medicine

Match each definition with the correct term. Write the letter in the space provided.

_____11. drugs sold without a prescription
because they are often used to
treat minor problems

_____12. any substance used to treat
disease, injury, or pain

_____13. medicine that can be bought only if a doctor orders its use

a. medicine
b. prescription medicine
c. over-the-counter
medicine

Lesson: Drug Misuse and Abuse

14. Any use of a medicine that is different from the intended use is

_____ .

15. When taking medicine, what four rules should you follow?

_____

_____

_____

_____

16. What is drug abuse?

_____

_____

_____

Lesson: Drug Addiction

_____ **17.** The pleasant effects that some drugs produce can cause people to
want to
a. use the drug over and over.
b. never use the drug again.
c. use a different drug.
d. stop using drugs.

_____ **18.** Which of the following is a symptom of psychological withdrawal?
a. sleeplessness
b. irritability
c. depression
d. All of the above

Name _____ Class _____ Date _____

Concept Review *continued*

19. What is drug addiction?

_____

_____

_____

Match each definition with the correct term. Write the letter in the space provided.

_____ **20.** the negative symptoms that result when a drug-dependent person stops taking a drug

_____ **21.** the uncontrollable use of a drug

_____ **22.** the need for a drug in order to function properly

_____ **23.** the body's chemical need for a drug

_____ **24.** a person's emotional or mental need for a drug

a. drug addiction
b. withdrawal
c. physical dependence
d. psychological dependence
e. dependence

Lesson: The Consequences of Drug Abuse

25. List the five types of problems that can arise because of drug abuse or addiction.

_____

_____

_____

_____

_____

26. Teenagers who abuse or become addicted to drugs lose

_____ in activities that were once important to them.

27. A person who abuses drugs will have difficulty _____ and he or she may forget from one day to the next what happened in class.

28. To a person with a drug problem, respecting others'

_____ is less important than getting drugs.

_____**29.** Permanent brain damage and mental problems are two possible effects
drugs may have on the
   a. heart.
   b. lungs.
   c. nervous system.
   d. blood.

Lesson: Stimulants and Depressants

_____**30.** Which of the following is NOT a danger of using stimulants?
   a. heart failure
   b. strengthened heart muscles
   c. brain damage
   d. stroke

_____**31.** The most commonly used depressant is
   a. alcohol
   b. Valium
   c. Xanax
   d. nicotine

32. Any drug that causes activity in the body and brain to slow is called a

_____.

33. Any drug that speeds up the activity of the body and the brain is a

_____.

Lesson: Marijuana

34. Marijuana is the dried leaves and flowers of the _____
plant.

35. The active chemical in marijuana is called _____.

36. List three possible effects of marijuana.

_____

_____

_____

37. Marijuana affects _____ and the ability to react quickly.

38. People who are _____ dependent on marijuana are often
irritable or unable to sleep if they do not use the drug.

_____ **39.** Which of the following is a problem of long-term use of marijuana?
    a. coughing
    b. frequent colds
    c. lung cancer
    d. All of the above

Lesson: Hallucinogens and Inhalants

Match each definition with the correct term. Write the letter in the space provided.

_____ **40.** a drug that causes a person to sense things that don't actually exist

_____ **41.** a sudden reliving of the hallucinogen experience

_____ **42.** a drug that is inhaled directly and enters the bloodstream through the lungs

    a. hallucinogen
    b. inhalant
    c. flashback

43. Physical reactions to hallucinogens may include nausea, increased heart rate,

increased _____, and sweating.

44. Because inhalants prevent _____ from reaching your

brain, inhalants damage your brain with each use.

Lesson: Staying Drug Free

45. List four reasons to remain drug free.

_____

_____

_____

_____

46. To stay drug free, learn ways to handle _____ in your life
so you won't feel tempted to try to feel better by using drugs.

47. To stay drug free, get involved in _____ service by
volunteering at a local day care center or animal shelter.

_____ **48.** Which of the following is NOT a way to stay drug free?
    a. Participate in sports.
    b. Develop a hobby.
    c. Make friends with people who use drugs.
    d. Stay connected to a trusted adult.

Activity

Health Inventory

Teens and Drugs

Answer the following questions to help you evaluate how well you stack up as a user of medicines. Write *yes* or *no* in the space to the left of each statement.

_____ **1.** Can you name every medication that you currently take?

_____ **2.** Do you read the label and follow the directions on each OTC medication that you use?

_____ **3.** Are you personally aware of whether or not you have allergies to any medications? If you do have any allergies to medication, can you name the medication?

_____ **4.** Have you ever asked your doctor or pharmacist for information or advice regarding the choices of an OTC medication or about a medicine that had been prescribed for you?

_____ **5.** Have you ever looked for information about medicine in an Internet resource? Can you name the resource?

_____ **6.** Do you say no or walk away whenever someone suggests using illegal drugs?

_____ **7.** Do you know the signs of drug addiction and where to go for help if you think someone has a problem?

SCORE YOURSELF

Give yourself one point for each *yes* answer. Write your score here _____.

6–7: You follow good practices for wise use of medicines.

4–5: You have some knowledge of how to use medicines wisely, but you should try to gain more knowledge.

0–3: There are some important gaps in your understanding of good practices for wise use of medicines in your life. You need to take responsibility for learning more about using medicines.

Activity

Health Behavior Contract

Teens and Drugs

My Goals: I, _____, will accomplish one or more of the following goals:

I will use medicines properly.

I will avoid situations in which I might be pressured to use drugs.

I will refuse drugs if they are offered to me.

Other: _____

_____

My Reasons: By using medicines properly I will avoid many health problems, such as drug abuse and addiction. By avoiding situations in which I may be pressured to use drugs and by refusing drugs if they are offered to me, I can protect myself from the problems that are caused by drug use.

Other: _____

_____

My Values: Personal values that will help me meet my goals are

_____

_____

_____

My Plan: The actions I will take to meet my goals are

_____

_____

_____

Evaluation: I will use my Health Journal to keep a log of actions I took to fulfill this contract. After 1 month, I will evaluate my goals. I will adjust my plan if my goals are not being met. If my goals are being met, I will consider setting additional goals.

Signed _____

Date _____

Activity

Life Skills: Being a Wise Consumer

Lesson: Using Drugs
TAKING DRUGS ORALLY

To take a drug orally, means to take it through the mouth. Swallowing, chewing, and drinking are all ways of taking drugs orally. Drugs that can be taken orally come in the form of pills, capsules, or liquid. Pills, sometimes called tablets, are medicine in a solid form. Capsules are tiny containers that hold a drug in powdered or liquid form.

Choose one over-the counter cold medicine that comes in both a solid form, such as pills or capsules, and a liquid form. Study the label for each form, and answer the questions below.

1. What is the advantage of the liquid form of the medication over the solid form?

_____

_____

_____

2. Is the dosage for children the same or different for the liquid form versus the solid form? Does the dosage for the two forms of medicine differ for adults?

_____

_____

_____

3. Are the warnings for children on the labels the same or different for the liquid form versus the solid form? Do the warnings differ for adults?

_____

_____

_____

4. What is the dosage of each form for adults? What is the dosage of each form for children?

_____

_____

_____

Activity

Life Skills: Coping

Lesson: Hallucinogens and Inhalants
COPING WITH THE STRESS OF PEER PRESSURE

Peer pressure can be extremely stressful, but you can learn to cope with it. Consider the following situation. Then, decide what you would do.

Last period art class is always fun. Bill and Alicia are laughing in the dark room where you develop photographs. You look into the room to see what's so funny. Bill and Alicia are inhaling glue fumes. Later, both Bill and Alicia are caught by the photography teacher. When your parents hear about the incident, they tell you that they do not want you to hang out with anyone who is sniffing glue.

How would you cope with this incident? How would you relate to your friends, Bill and Alicia, and also obey your parents? Describe two ways that the situation could turn, one in your favor and one against.

_____

_____

_____

_____

_____

_____

_____

_____

_____

_____

_____

_____

_____

_____

_____

Skills Worksheet)

Concept Review

Lesson: What Is an Infectious Disease?

1. Any illness caused by a microorganism is called a(n)

_____ disease.

2. An illness that can spread directly from one person to another person is

called a(n) _____ disease.

3. Describe four ways that infections are spread.

_____

_____

_____

_____

4. What are three examples of infectious diseases?

_____

_____

_____

Lesson: Bacterial Infections

Use the following terms to complete the paragraph below: *dividing, cells, deadly, host, microorganisms, bacterial, antibiotic, damage, infection, nutrients,* **and** *untreated.*

5. _____ infections are caused by bacteria, which are simple

single-celled **6.** _____. Bacteria reproduce quickly by

7. _____ in half. This is why the presence of only a few

bacteria in the beginning can result in a(n) **8.** _____ very

rapidly. First, bacteria invade a(n) **9.** _____, such as a human,

animal, or plant. Once inside, the bacteria get **10.** _____ from

the host's **11.** _____. During this process, the bacteria may

cause serious **12.** _____ to the host. A bacterial infection,

if left **13.** _____, can become very serious or even

| Concept Review *continued*

14. _____. A bacterial infection can be treated with

a(n) **15.** _____.

16. Describe five ways you can reduce your chances of getting a bacterial infection.

_____

_____

_____

_____

_____

Match the bacterial infection with its symptoms. Write the letter in the space provided.

_____ **17.** strep throat

_____ **18.** sinus infection

_____ **19.** tuberculosis

a. congestion, runny nose, fever, headache

b. fever, night sweats, cough

c. fever, body aches, pain when swallowing

Lesson: Viral Infections

In the blanks provided, write *V* beside the items that describe a virus. Write *NV* beside the items that do NOT describe a virus.

_____ **20.** can be passed by insect bites

_____ **21.** not considered alive by scientists

_____ **22.** cannot be fought by the body's own defenses

_____ **23.** causes a bacterial infection

_____ **24.** can reproduce on its own

_____ **25.** can sometimes be prevented with a vaccine

26. What is a vaccine? How can it help prevent viral diseases?

_____

_____

_____

_____

| Concept Review *continued*

Complete the chart.

VIRAL INFECTION	SYMPTOMS (Give 3 for each.)	HOW IT IS SPREAD (Give 3 for each.)
Common Cold	27.	28.
Influenza	29.	30.
Mononucleosis	31.	32.

Lesson: Sexually Transmitted Diseases

33. What is a sexually transmitted disease?

_____

_____

34. List three possible consequences of STDs.

_____

_____

35. Describe four ways that HIV can spread from person to person.

_____

_____

_____

_____

| Concept Review *continued*

Match each item in the right column to the correct term in the left column. Write the letter in the space provided.

_____**36.** the only 100% effective way to protect yourself from STDs

_____**37.** can cause mental illness, heart damage, and death

_____**38.** can cause cervical cancer and deformities in unborn children

_____**39.** can cause sterility or pregnancy complications

_____**40.** is the virus that causes AIDS

_____**41.** has been linked to an increased risk of HIV infection

_____**42.** often causes genital warts and can cause cervical cancer

_____**43.** can cause fever, weight loss, and body sores

a. HIV

b. AIDS

c. sexual abstinence

d. genital herpes

e. trichomoniasis

f. chlamydia

g. syphilis

h. human papilloma virus (HPV)

Match the name of each STD in the left column with its treatment or cure in the right column. Write the letter in the space provided. One answer will be used twice.

_____**44.** AIDS

_____**45.** chlamydia

_____**46.** human papilloma virus

_____**47.** genital herpes

_____**48.** gonorrhea

_____**49.** syphilis

_____**50.** trichomoniasis

a. warts can be removed; no cure

b. treated with antiviral medicines; no cure

c. cured with medication

d. some strains can be cured with antibiotics

e. cured with antibiotics

f. treated with combinations of drugs; no cure

| Concept Review *continued*

Lesson: Preventing the Spread of Infectious Diseases

51. What is the most common way that infectious diseases are spread?

_____

_____

52. The best way to prevent the spread of contagious infections is to practice

good _____.

53. Always wash your _____ before you eat and every time

you use the bathroom.

54. _____ on your hands can infect you when you touch your

face or when you eat.

55. You should always wash with _____ and

_____.

56. Why is it important to shower regularly?

_____

_____

57. What are three ways to protect yourself from infectious diseases?

_____

_____

_____

58. What are three ways to protect others from infectious diseases?

_____

_____

_____

Activity

Health Inventory

Infectious Diseases

Decide how well each of the following statements applies to your knowledge or behaviors. Read each statement and check the appropriate box.

Strongly applies	Applies somewhat	Does not apply at all		
❏	❏	❏	**1.**	I wash my hands after using the rest room.
❏	❏	❏	**2.**	I shower often with soap and warm water.
❏	❏	❏	**3.**	I do not share food or drinks with other people.
❏	❏	❏	**4.**	I cover my mouth and nose with a tissue when I sneeze or cough.
❏	❏	❏	**5.**	I know that the only sure way to prevent the spread of STDs is to practice abstinence.
❏	❏	❏	**6.**	I know that bacteria and viruses cause infectious diseases.
❏	❏	❏	**7.**	I use soap when I wash my hands.
❏	❏	❏	**8.**	I wash my hands for at least 20 seconds.
❏	❏	❏	**9.**	When I wash my hands, I am careful to clean my fingernails.
❏	❏	❏	**10.**	I limit my contact with people whom I suspect may have a contagious infection.
❏	❏	❏	**11.**	When I suspect that I may have an infectious illness, I visit my doctor so I can begin any necessary treatment.
❏	❏	❏	**12.**	I know that many illnesses, if left untreated, can lead to dangerous consequences.
❏	❏	❏	**13.**	I eat properly.
❏	❏	❏	**14.**	I get enough sleep.

Score yourself: Give yourself 3 points for each *strongly applies* answer, 1 point for each *applies somewhat*, and 0 for each *does not apply at all*. Write your score here _____.

33–42: Excellent—You definitely understand infectious diseases, how they spread, and how to protect yourself and others from them.

23–32: Good—You mostly understand infectious diseases, how they spread, and how to protect yourself and others from them.

11–22: Fair—You may need to put more effort into protecting yourself and others from the spread of infectious diseases.

0–10: Learning more about infectious diseases will help you to protect yourself and others from their spread.

Name _____   Class _____   Date _____

Health Behavior Contract

Infectious Diseases

My Goals: I, _____, will accomplish one or more of the following goals:

I will practice good hygiene.

I will exercise regularly, eat a healthy diet, and get plenty of sleep.

I will ask my parents or doctor about my vaccination record.

Other: _____

_____

My Reasons: By practicing good hygiene, I will avoid catching and spreading many diseases. By exercising regularly, eating a healthy diet, and getting enough sleep, I will help protect my body from disease. By asking about my vaccination record, I will find out whether I need vaccines or vaccine boosters.

Other: _____

_____

My Values: Personal values that will help me meet my goals are

_____

_____

_____

My Plan: The actions I will take to meet my goals are

_____

_____

_____

Evaluation: I will use my Health Journal to keep a log of actions I took to fulfill this contract. After 1 month, I will evaluate my goals. I will adjust my plan if my goals are not being met. If my goals are being met, I will consider setting additional goals.

Signed _____

Date _____

Activity

Life Skills: Being a Wise Consumer

Lesson: Viral Infections
COMPARING COLD AND FLU REMEDIES

When it comes to treating viral infections, especially the common cold and the flu, there is a wide assortment of remedies available. While there is nothing that you can buy at a store to *cure* a viral infection, there are many products that can help treat the symptoms of these infections.

Visit a local pharmacy or the pharmacy aisle at a local grocery store. Locate the cold and flu remedies. Look at various remedies for cold and flu symptoms.

Follow the directions below to complete the chart on the following page.

1. **Write a short description of each product**. Include here whether the product is being sold as a flu remedy, a cold remedy, a flu and cold remedy, or a treatment for a specific symptom, such as a cough.

2. **Write the brand name of the product**. If it is a generic or store brand, write *generic*.

3. **List the symptoms that the product claims to treat**. These symptoms are usually listed on the front of the package, but you may have to look at the back, under *Active Ingredients*.

4. **Write the price of the product**. If the product is on sale, write the sale price.

5. **Write the number of doses in the package**. Use the regular adult dose. For example, if the instructions on the package say that an adult should take two tablets every four hours, that is a dose of 2 tablets. Divide the total number of tablets by 2 to find out how many doses are in the package.

6. **Evaluate the value of this product**. Consider the price, the symptoms it treats, and the number of doses per package. Rate the value of this product, using the rating *Excellent, Very Good, Good, Fair,* or *Poor*. Your rating should reflect your opinion of the price value as well as the usefulness of the product.

Name _____ Class _____ Date _____

PRODUCT	BRAND	SYMPTOMS	PRICE	DOSES	VALUE
cough syrup	generic	cough	$2.29	15	Very Good

1. For the products that you rated *Excellent*, briefly explain your reasons.

_____

_____

_____

_____

2. For the products that you rated *Poor*, briefly explain your reasons.

_____

_____

_____

_____

_____

_____

Activity

Life Skills: Practicing Wellness

Lesson: Preventing the Spread of Infectious Diseases
TAKING ACTION TO AVOID INFECTION

Read the following situations. For each situation, describe the action or actions you should take in order to reduce your chances of catching or spreading an infection. For each action you describe, explain why it will help prevent the spread of infectious diseases. Write your answers on the lines provided.

1. You are about to sneeze.

_____

_____

_____

_____

2. You use a public telephone.

_____

_____

_____

_____

3. Your doctor has told you that you have a cold.

_____

_____

_____

_____

_____

4. You use a public restroom.

_____

_____

_____

_____

_____

5. You have just finished helping pick up litter at a local park.

_____

_____

_____

6. You find out that a classmate has the flu.

_____

_____

_____

_____

7. You are about to eat a sandwich for lunch.

_____

_____

_____

_____

8. You shake hands with a neighbor. As he walks away, you hear him cough several times.

_____

_____

_____

_____

9. A friend offers you a bite of his apple.

_____

_____

_____

_____

Skills Worksheet

Concept Review

Lesson: Noninfectious Diseases and Body Systems

Match each noninfectious disease listed below with its cause. Write the letter in the space provided. One cause will not be used.

_____ 1. brain injury

_____ 2. cystic fibrosis

_____ 3. diabetes

_____ 4. asthma

_____ 5. anemia

_____ 6. high blood pressure

a. hereditary

b. multiple causes

c. immune defect

d. nutritional defect

e. accident

f. congenital

g. metabolic disorder

7. A disease not caused by a virus or living organism is

_____.

8. A(n) _____ is two or more tissues working together.

9. A(n) _____ is two or more organs that work together.

10. A(n) _____ is a harmful change in your body's normal activities.

Lesson: Circulatory System

Match the parts of the circulatory system with their function. Write the letter in the space provided. One part will not be used.

_____ 11. receives low-oxygen blood from all parts of the body

_____ 12. pumps low-oxygen blood to the lungs

_____ 13. exchange of low-oxygen blood for high-oxygen blood

_____ 14. receives high-oxygen blood from the lungs

_____ 15. pumps high-oxygen blood to all parts of the body

_____ 16. carries blood to the heart

_____ 17. carries blood from the heart

a. left atrium

b. right atrium

c. to the rest of the body

d. right ventricle

e. in the lungs

f. left ventricle

g. veins

h. arteries

18. A _____ happens when the heart does not receive enough blood.

19. A condition in which the pressure inside your large arteries is too high is _____.

20. A heart murmur is a _____ that happens at birth.

21. A disease in which your body does not produce enough red blood cells is _____.

Lesson: Respiratory System

Fill in the blanks to complete the sentences using the following terms: *alveoli, carbon dioxide, asthma, oxygen, emphysema,* **and** *lungs.*

22. Your nose and mouth, trachea, bronchi, and bronchioles carry air that you breathe to the _____.

23. The lungs have many small air sacs called _____.

24. A gas from the air, called _____, passes through the air sacs into your blood.

25. A gas from your blood, called _____, passes through the alveoli into the air in your lungs.

26. The disease _____ causes the bronchioles in the lungs to narrow.

27. A disease called _____ causes the alveoli to become thin and stretched.

Lesson: Nervous System

28. Name two signs of Alzheimer's disease.

_____

_____

_____

_____

| Concept Review *continued*

29. How does Parkinson's disease affect the body?

_____

_____

_____

_____

_____

Fill in the blanks using the following terms to show how different parts of the nervous system work together: *heart rate, peripheral, central nervous system, autonomic, muscles,* **and** *somatic.*

The brain and spinal cord make up the **30.** _____.

All the nerves outside the brain and spinal cord are known as the

31. _____ nervous system, which has two main parts, the

32. _____ nervous system, which controls body functions

such as digestion and **33.** _____, and the

34. _____ nervous system which sends information between

the bones, **35.** _____, and skin.

Lesson: Endocrine System

Match each of the glands of the endocrine system with the function of the hormone it produces. Write the letter of the correct answer in the space provided.

_____**36.** produces growth hormone

_____**37.** produces insulin

_____**38.** control(s) female sexual development

_____**39.** produces hormones for salt metabolism

_____**40.** control(s) male sexual development

_____**41.** produces hormones necessary for growth and
metabolism

a. ovaries
b. adrenal
c. pituitary
d. testes
e. pancreas
f. thyroid

42. When a person has _____, the body produces little or no
insulin.

Name _____ Class _____ Date _____

| Concept Review *continued*

43. When a person has _____, the thyroid gland produces too much of its hormone, which speeds up metabolism.

44. When a person has _____, the body makes insulin but cannot use it properly.

Lesson: Digestive System

Match each part of the digestive system with its function. Write the letter in the space provided.

_____**45.** where digestion of food is completed and nutrients absorbed

_____**46.** where digestion begins

_____**47.** holds food and partially digests it

_____**48.** where water from digested food is absorbed

_____**49.** where undigested and unabsorbed food leaves the body

a. anus
b. large intestine
c. mouth
d. stomach
e. small intestine

50. The disease of the digestive system that makes a person allergic to gluten is

_____.

51. A disease that attacks the lining of the intestines and causes diarrhea, cramps,

and fever is called _____.

Lesson: Urinary System

Match each part of the urinary system with its function. Write the letter of the correct answer in the space provided.

_____**52.** millions of tiny filters that constantly clean blood in the kidneys

_____**53.** carries urine away from the kidneys

_____**54.** made of waste products and water from the blood

_____**55.** organs that remove wastes and water from your blood

_____**56.** slender tube through which urine leaves your body

a. urethra
b. ureters
c. nephrons
d. urine
e. kidneys

       Noninfectious Diseases and Disorders

| Concept Review *continued*

57. A kidney disease in which sugar damages the nephrons so they cannot filter

wastes is called _____.

58. A hereditary disease in which cysts replace the nephrons is called

_____.

59. A circulatory disease which also destroys the nephrons is called

_____.

Lesson: Skin, Bones, and Muscles

Match each disease of the skin, bones, or muscles with its cause. Write the letter in the space provided.

_____ **60.** exposure to sunlight

_____ **61.** hereditary disease of muscles

_____ **62.** loss of bone density

_____ **63.** skin disease with unknown cause

_____ **64.** lack of vitamin D

a. psoriasis
b. rickets
c. skin cancer
d. muscular dystrophy
e. osteoporosis

Complete each sentence below to show that you understand how your skin, bones, and muscles work together.

65. If I had muscles and bones, but no skin,

_____

_____

66. If I had skin and muscles, but no bones,

_____

_____

67. If I had skin and bones, but no muscles,

_____

_____

| Concept Review *continued*

Lesson: Eyes and Ears

Use the numbers *1* through *6* to place the following steps in the order that they happen to allow you to hear.

_____**68.** electrical impulses sent to the brain

_____**69.** vibrations of the eardrum

_____**70.** converts vibrations to electrical impulses

_____**71.** sound waves in the air

_____**72.** hearing occurs

_____**73.** vibrations of bones in middle ear

Match the function with the organ that helps in the process of seeing. Write the letter in the space provided. One term will not be used.

_____**74.** changes electrical impulses to images

_____**75.** let light into the eye

_____**76.** carries electrical impulses to the brain

_____**77.** focuses light on the retina

a. lens

b. optic nerve

c. cornea, pupil, lens

d. brain

e. retina

78. A disease that causes high pressure in the fluid inside the eye is

_____ .

79. What is a cataract?

_____

_____

_____

80. List four causes of deafness.

_____

_____

_____

_____

Activity

Health Inventory

Noninfectious Diseases and Disorders

Use the checklist below to learn about how you take care of your skin, bones, and muscles. Put a check in the box next to each statement that describes you.

❑ **1.** I take care of a cut in my skin as soon as it happens.

❑ **2.** I keep my skin clean to avoid infection.

❑ **3.** I always use sunscreen when I'm exposed to the sun during summer.

❑ **4.** I avoid being in the sun between 10 A.M. and 2 P.M. during summer.

❑ **5.** I always wear a cap when I'm exposed to the sun during summer.

❑ **6.** I always use protective equipment when doing contact sports.

❑ **7.** I always use a helmet when riding a bike.

❑ **8.** I always use a seatbelt when riding in a car.

❑ **9.** I avoid jumping from high places.

❑ **10.** I take care of my muscles by getting plenty of exercise every day.

❑ **11.** I take care of every injury as soon as possible.

❑ **12.** I drink milk to keep my bones strong.

Give yourself one point for each checkmark. Write your score here _____.

10–12: You're taking good care of your skin, bones, and muscles.
6–9: You know some of the facts about caring for your skin, bones, and muscles.
Below 6: You can take better care of your skin, bones, and muscles. Try harder.

Name _____ Class _____ Date _____

Health Behavior Contract

Noninfectious Diseases and Disorders

My Goals: I, _____, will accomplish one or more of the following goals:

I will identify three behaviors that may put me at risk of developing a noninfectious disease.

I will create a plan to change my health behaviors that put me at risk of developing a noninfectious disease.

Other: _____

_____

My Reasons: By changing my behavior and lowering my risk of developing a noninfectious disease, I will be healthier and will not miss out on things I want to do. I will be able to participate in activities at school, with my family, and with my friends.

Other: _____

_____

My Values: Personal values that will help me meet my goals are

_____

_____

My Plan: The actions I will take to meet my goals are

_____

_____

_____

Evaluation: I will use my Health Journal to keep a log of actions I took to fulfill this contract. After 1 month, I will evaluate my goals. I will adjust my plan if my goals are not being met. If my goals are being met, I will consider setting additional goals.

Signed _____

Date _____

Activity

Life Skills: Practicing Wellness

Lesson: Circulatory System
KEEPING YOUR HEART HEALTHY

Sometimes in the news, you hear about someone young and famous who becomes ill or dies. News like that may make you stop to think about how you can improve your own health. As an example, your circulatory system helps keep you alive and well. Many young people think that only older people have to worry about their heart and blood vessels. However, younger people can help maintain a healthy circulatory system by practicing the following good health habits: eating nutritious food with not too much fat, getting plenty of exercise, not being over-weight, and not smoking.

Follow these guidelines to help you achieve and maintain a healthy circulatory system.

1. **How can you be sure you are eating a healthy diet?** Control the amount of fatty food you eat to keep your blood vessels healthy. Increase your consumption of fruit and vegetables.

2. **Get advice about the most beneficial exercises for your heart.** Exercise increases the pumping ability of the heart.

3. **Find out how exercise affects your blood vessels.** It reduces the amount of fat in the blood and increases the number of blood vessels. It can also help you maintain your proper weight.

4. **How does smoking harm the heart?** Smoking causes high blood pressure, which harms the blood vessels and makes blood flow more difficult.

5. **Make a list of ways you intend to improve your health habits.** Share your list with others.

1. Write down two ways in which you can improve the health of your circulatory system.

   _____

   _____

   _____

2. Write down two reasons why you want to improve the health of your circulatory system.

   _____

   _____

   _____

Activity

Life Skills: Setting Goals

Lesson: Skin, Bones, and Muscles
CREATING AN EXERCISE PLAN

When the astronauts go to the International Space Station, they spend many hours doing physical exercise to keep their bones and muscles fit. Your bones and muscles also need exercise. In the space below, create an exercise program. Keep in mind the following guidelines to help you achieve and maintain physical fitness.

- **Appraise your present physical fitness.** Write down the kinds of exercise you do now. How often and how long do you exercise at the present time?

- **Get advice about the most beneficial exercises for you.** Which of these exercises will increase your heart rate and stretch your muscles?

- **Make a reasonable schedule for your daily exercise.** What can you do to ensure that you will keep to your schedule? What will you do on days when it is impossible to exercise?

- **Set goals that you are determined to achieve.** Draw up an exercise plan to help you meet your goals with a family member or someone who can help keep you on track.

- **Try to interest a family member or friend to share your exercise routine.** Why is it helpful to exercise with someone else?

_____

_____

_____

_____

_____

_____

_____

_____

_____

_____

_____

Skills Worksheet

Concept Review

Lesson: What Makes You You

1. Where do your genes come from?

_____

_____

_____

2. How does your environment affect your growth and development?

_____

_____

_____

Match each item in the right column to the correct term in the left column. Write the letter in the space provided.

_____ **3.** a cell that contains half the genes of the parent

_____ **4.** passing of traits from parents to children

_____ **5.** the instructions for how you will grow and develop

_____ **6.** the people and places around you

a. genes

b. environment

c. heredity

d. sex cell

Lesson: The Male Reproductive System

Match each item in the right column to the correct term in the left column. Write the letter in the space provided.

_____ **7.** sex cell provided by the male

_____ **8.** organ in which sperm mature

_____ **9.** organs that produce testosterone

_____ **10.** a tube that runs through the penis

a. urethra

b. testes

c. epididymis

d. sperm

11. List four problems of the male reproductive system.

_____

_____

_____

12. What are four ways to protect the health of the male reproductive system?

_____

_____

_____

_____

_____

_____

_____

Lesson: The Female Reproductive System

In the blanks provided, fill in the letters of the term or phrase being described.

13. sex cell produced by women: O __U __ or E __ __

14. process in which a mature egg is released: __ __ U __ __ T __ __ N

15. organ in which eggs are stored: __ V __ R __

16. organ that holds a fetus during pregnancy: __ T __ R __ S

17. monthly shedding of the endometrium: __E __ S T __ U __ __ I __ __

| Concept Review *continued*

18. Describe what happens in the typical menstrual cycle on the following days:

   a. days 1–13

   _____

   _____

   b. day 14

   _____

   _____

   c. days 15–17

   _____

   _____

   d. days 18–28

   _____

   _____

19. Name four problems that can affect the female reproductive system.

   _____

   _____

   _____

   _____

20. Name five strategies to protect the health of the female reproductive system.

   _____

   _____

   _____

   _____

Lesson: The Endocrine System

21. What is a hormone?

   _____

   _____

22. What do hormones regulate?

_____

_____

23. What is a gland?

_____

_____

24. Describe the two main functions of the endocrine system.

_____

_____

Lesson: Growing Up

Match each definition with the correct term. Write the letter in the space provided. Some terms will not be used.

_____**25.** the time when a woman is carrying a developing baby in her uterus

_____**26.** a developing human from fertilization until the eighth week of pregnancy

_____**27.** three specific time periods during pregnancy

a. embryo

b. fetus

c. pregnancy

d. trimesters

28. A developing human from the ninth week of pregnancy until birth is called

a(n) _____.

29. Describe the development of a human during the first 12 weeks of pregnancy.

_____

_____

_____

_____

_____

_____

_____

Concept Review *continued*

30. Name two developments that usually occur during each of the following stages of childhood:

a. infancy

_____

_____

b. early childhood

_____

_____

c. middle childhood

_____

_____

d. late childhood

_____

_____

Lesson: Becoming an Adult

31. Define the term *adolescence*.

_____

_____

32. Define *puberty*.

_____

_____

33. Describe three ways humans prepare for adulthood during adolescence.

_____

_____

_____

34. What is adulthood?

_____

_____

▌Concept Review *continued*

35. Describe three responsibilities of adults.

_____

_____

_____

_____

_____

36. Describe two positive aspects of aging.

_____

_____

_____

_____

_____

37. A deep feeling of sadness about a loss is called _____.

38. Name the 5 stages of grief.

_____

_____

_____

_____

_____

Activity

Health Inventory

Your Changing Body

Read each of the statements below. Think about how well each statement describes your behavior. Then, write *always*, *sometimes*, or *never* in the space next to each statement.

_____ **1.** I bathe every day.

_____ **2.** I don't wear tight or damp clothing longer than I have to.

_____ **3.** I ask my parents if I have a question about my development.

_____ **4.** I see a doctor for any problems with my reproductive system.

_____ **5.** I practice abstinence to avoid STDs.

_____ **6.** I wear proper safety equipment when I play sports.

_____ **7.** I perform regular self-examinations.

_____ **8.** I maintain good hygiene.

_____ **9.** I am aware of changes in my body.

Score yourself on this quiz. Give yourself 2 points for each *always*, 1 point for each *sometimes*, and 0 points for each *never*. Write your score here _____.

12–18: Excellent—You have learned how to protect the health of your reproductive system.

7–11: Good—You have made some choices that will protect the health of your reproductive system.

0–6: Fair—You may benefit from learning more about how to protect the health of your reproductive system.

Activity

Health Behavior Contract

Your Changing Body

My Goals: I, _____, will accomplish one or
more of the following goals:

I will protect my reproductive system from harm.

I will practice preventive healthcare.

Other: _____

_____

My Reasons: By protecting my reproductive health, I will protect my overall
health. By practicing preventive healthcare, I will protect my reproductive system
and other body systems from injury or illness.

Other: _____

_____

My Values: Personal values that will help me meet my goals are

_____

_____

_____

My Plan: The actions I will take to meet my goals are

_____

_____

_____

Evaluation: I will use my Health Journal to keep a log of actions I took to fulfill
this contract. After 1 month, I will evaluate my goals. I will adjust my plan if my
goals are not being met. If my goals are being met, I will consider setting additional goals.

Signed _____

Date _____

Activity

Life Skills: Practicing Wellness

Lesson: The Male Reproductive System
REPRODUCTIVE HEALTH

Regular visits to the doctor are an important part of wellness for men and boys. The health of the reproductive system can be monitored for problems during these check-ups, and any problems can be immediately treated. Find the following information using reliable research sources such as an encyclopedia and reputable Web sites, or interview a doctor or health care professional to obtain the information.

1. How often should men and boys see their doctor for regular checkups?

_____

_____

_____

_____

2. How do doctors monitor the health of the reproductive system of young boys?

_____

_____

_____

_____

_____

3. During puberty and adolescence, how does the doctor monitor the health of a young man's reproductive system?

_____

_____

_____

_____

4. What symptoms or conditions related to the reproductive system should prompt a male to seek medical attention from a healthcare professional?

_____

_____

_____

_____

Activity

Life Skills: Setting Goals

Lesson: Becoming an Adult
ADOLESCENCE

Adolescence is a time of growth and change. It is also a time to prepare for adult-hood. Although goals and interests change frequently during adolescence, some of the goals you set now will be lifetime goals. Think about the things that are most important to you. What goals can you set for your adult life based on your interests now? For example, if you are a wonderful babysitter, you might have a goal of becoming a preschool teacher.

1. What are some of your favorite interests and activities?

_____

_____

_____

2. Choose two of the interests and activities from question 1, and create goals for your adult life based on each of these interests.

_____

_____

_____

_____

_____

_____

3. What actions can you take in the next year that will help you to reach these goals? List two actions for each goal.

_____

_____

_____

_____

_____

_____

Skills Worksheet

Concept Review

Lesson: Injury Prevention at Home and at School

Write the letter of the correct answer in the space provided.

_____ 1. What should you do if you find a gun?
  a. Check to see if it is loaded.
  b. Walk away, and tell an adult.
  c. Walk away, and don't tell anyone.
  d. Take the gun to an adult.

_____ 2. Which of the following is NOT a good safety tip?
  a. Act before you think.
  b. Be aware of your surroundings.
  c. Know your limits.
  d. Practice refusal skills.

3. List four common types of accidents that can happen at home.

_____

_____

4. List three items that can cause injury during a lab class.

_____

_____

5. List five ways to avoid violence.

_____

_____

_____

_____

_____

Match the definitions with the correct term. Write the letter in the space provided.

_____ **6.** an unexpected event that may lead to injury

_____ **7.** a group of people who often use violence

_____ **8.** the use of physical force to hurt someone or cause damage

  a. accident
  b. gang
  c. violence

| Concept Review *continued*

Lesson: Fire Safety
Write the letter of the correct answer in the space provided.

_____ **9.** What can you use to put out a small fire?
  a. fire extinguisher
  b. baking soda
  c. salt
  d. All of the above

10. A(n) _____ is an alarm that detects smoke from a fire.

11. A(n) _____ is a device that releases chemicals to put out a fire.

Lesson: Safety on the Road
Write the letter of the correct answer in the space provided.

_____ **12.** Which of the following is NOT a good safety tip?
  a. Cross the street at a crosswalk.
  b. Don't wear headphones when you're walking.
  c. Walk facing away from traffic.
  d. Wear bright or reflective clothing if you must walk after dark.

_____ **13.** How can you stay safer when riding a bus?
  a. Cross the street behind the bus.
  b. Learn where the emergency exits are located.
  c. Stand up while the bus is moving.
  d. All of the above

14. Explain why you should wear a helmet when cycling and skating.

_____

_____

_____

15. Explain why you should wear a seat belt when riding in a car.

_____

_____

_____

| Concept Review *continued*

Lesson: Safety Outdoors

16. What are five ways to stay safer when hiking and camping?

_____

_____

_____

_____

_____

17. What are five ways to stay safer when skiing or snowboarding?

_____

_____

_____

_____

_____

Match the definitions with the correct term. Write the letter in the space provided. One term will not be used.

_____ **18.** a below-normal body temperature

_____ **19.** damage to the skin and other tissues caused by extreme cold

_____ **20.** a condition caused by too much water loss through sweating on a hot day

_____ **21.** an injury that happens when the body cannot control its temperature

a. frostbite

b. sunburn

c. heatstroke

d. heat exhaustion

e. hypothermia

Lesson: Natural Disasters

22. Explain how you can prepare for a natural disaster.

_____

_____

_____

_____

| Concept Review *continued*

Match the definitions with the correct term. Write the letter in the space provided. One term will not be used.

_____ **23.** a natural event that causes widespread injury, death, and property damage

_____ **24.** a shaking of the Earth's surface caused by movement along a break in the Earth's crust

_____ **25.** a large, spinning tropical weather system with wind speeds of at least 74 miles per hour

_____ **26.** an overflowing of water into areas that are normally dry

_____ **27.** a forecast that tells people that severe weather has developed

_____ **28.** a forecast that tells people that severe weather may happen

_____ **29.** a flood that rises and falls with little or no warning

_____ **30.** a spinning column of air that has a high wind speed and touches the ground

a. hurricane

b. natural disaster

c. flood

d. tornado

e. warning

f. earthquake

g. thunderstorm

h. watch

i. flash flood

Lesson: Deciding to Give First Aid

31. What are the three steps for handling an emergency?

_____

_____

32. What are four things you should tell the operator when making an emergency phone call?

_____

_____

_____

_____

| Concept Review *continued*

33. A(n) _____ is a sudden event that demands immediate action.

34. _____ is emergency medical care for someone who has been hurt or who is sick.

Lesson: Abdominal Thrusts and Rescue Breathing

Write the letter of the correct answer in the space provided.

_____**35.** When an infant is choking,
  a. call for help, and start first aid.
  b. put your fingers in the infant's mouth to remove the object.
  c. push on the infant's stomach.
  d. All of the above

_____**36.** Cardiopulmonary resuscitation
  a. requires no special training.
  b. is used for victims who have a heart beat.
  c. is used for victims who aren't breathing and have no heart beat.
  d. is different from CPR.

37. Where do you place your fist when giving abdominal thrusts to an adult?

_____

_____

38. What should you do before starting rescue breathing on an adult?

_____

_____

_____

_____

39. How does rescue breathing for small children differ from rescue breathing for adults?

_____

_____

_____

| Concept Review *continued*

Lesson: First Aid for Injuries

Write the letter of the correct answer in the space provided.

_____ **40.** If someone gets a cut,
   a. stop the bleeding right away.
   b. put sterile gauze over the cut.
   c. use your hand to put pressure on the cut.
   d. All of the above

_____ **41.** If someone has a fracture,
   a. try to straighten it right away.
   b. don't use ice, because ice makes the swelling worse.
   c. call for help, and avoid moving the injured bone.
   d. All of the above

42. How should you care for a first-degree burn?

_____

_____

_____

43. How can you try to find out what someone has been poisoned by?

_____

_____

_____

44. Why shouldn't you move someone with a head, neck, or back injury?

_____

_____

_____

Match the definitions with the correct term. Write the letter in the space provided. One term will not be used.

_____ **45.** a broken or cracked bone

_____ **46.** an injury in which a bone has been forced out of the joint

_____ **47.** a burn in which the skin blisters, and the burn is very painful

a. dislocation

b. second-degree burn

c. fracture

d. third-degree burn

Activity

Health Inventory

Your Personal Safety

This checklist can help you assess how careful you are when walking or riding in a vehicle. Read the following questions. Then, check the appropriate box next to each one.

always	some-times	never	
❏	❏	❏	**1.** Do you walk on the sidewalk when one is available?
❏	❏	❏	**2.** Do you walk facing traffic?
❏	❏	❏	**3.** Do you cross the street at a crosswalk?
❏	❏	❏	**4.** Do you look both ways before crossing the street?
❏	❏	❏	**5.** Do you make sure the driver can see you if you're crossing in front of a vehicle?
❏	❏	❏	**6.** Do you try to avoid walking at night if you can?
❏	❏	❏	**7.** Do you avoid wearing headphones when walking?
❏	❏	❏	**8.** Do you wear a seat belt when riding in an automobile?
❏	❏	❏	**9.** Do you avoid distracting the driver when riding in a vehicle?
❏	❏	❏	**10.** Do you stay in your seat when riding in a vehicle?

SCORE YOURSELF

Give yourself 4 points for each *always* answer, 2 points for each *sometimes* answer, and 0 points for each *never* answer. Write your score here: _____.

40: Excellent—You do a great job of making safe decisions when walking or riding.

30–39: Very good—You need to make just a few small changes to be safer on the road.

20–29: Good—You are on the right track, but you need to make several changes.

10–19: Fair—You are taking too many risks when walking or riding, but you can change.

0–9: Poor—Luckily, it's not too late to change your behavior and keep yourself safer.

Name _____ Class _____ Date _____

Health Behavior Contract

Your Personal Safety

My Goals: I, _____, will accomplish one or more of the following goals:

I will learn how to avoid violence at school.

I will wear my seat belt.

I will take a first-aid class.

Other: _____

_____

My Reasons: Accidents can happen anywhere and at any time. Avoiding accidents, violence, and guns can keep me safer. Also, wearing my seat belt can save my life during an automobile accident. Learning first aid and CPR can help me save someone's life.

Other: _____

_____

My Values: Personal values that will help me meet my goals are

_____

_____

_____

My Plan: The actions I will take to meet my goals are

_____

_____

_____

Evaluation: I will use my Health Journal to keep a log of actions I took to fulfill this contract. After 1 month, I will evaluate my goals. I will adjust my plan if my goals are not being met. If my goals are being met, I will consider setting additional goals.

Signed _____

Date _____

Activity

Life Skills: Practicing Wellness

Lesson: Fire Safety
FIRE SAFETY AT HOME

Not all fires can be avoided, but many can. Use the following questions to help you evaluate the fire risks in your home.

Check *yes* or *no*.

yes	no	
❑	❑	**1.** Do family members leave the stove unattended when it is on?
❑	❑	**2.** Do you have any chemicals that can cause fires in your home?
❑	❑	**3.** Do you notice any other fire hazards in your home?
❑	❑	**4.** Do you have a smoke detector in every major room?
❑	❑	**5.** Do you have at least one fire extinguisher in your home?
❑	❑	**6.** Do you know what to do if a small fire starts?
❑	❑	**7.** Do you know how to put out a small grease fire?
❑	❑	**8.** Do you know what to do if a larger fire starts?
❑	❑	**9.** Do you know what number to dial for the fire department?
❑	❑	**10.** Does your family have an evacuation plan in case of fire?

ANALYSIS

1. What are some things you could do to help keep fires from starting?

_____

_____

_____

2. What are some things you could do to help detect a fire if it occurs?

_____

_____

_____

3. What are some things you could do to help you react more quickly in case of fire?

_____

_____

_____

Activity

Life Skills: Coping

Lesson: Natural Disasters
COPING WITH FEAR OF STORMS

Dorothy lives in Kansas, where tornadoes sometimes strike. One stormy afternoon, she is at home when she hears a warning on the radio. A tornado has been spotted close to her home. This frightens Dorothy. In the past, she has seen tornadoes pick up trees, bicycles, and even houses. But she knows what she should do. She grabs her little dog and heads for a safe place.

1. Dorothy lives in a house that doesn't have a basement or cellar. Where should she go in her house?

_____

_____

_____

2. What can Dorothy do to help herself stay calm while she waits for the storm to pass?

_____

_____

_____

3. On another day, Dorothy hears about a tornado that has touched down 100 miles from her home. What can she tell herself to keep from getting scared?

_____

_____

_____

4. Dorothy sometimes worries that she might be caught outside when a tornado is approaching. If that ever happens, what can she do to stay safe?

_____

_____

5. How does knowing what to do in case of a tornado help Dorothy cope with her fears?

_____

_____

_____